KIDS COOK
GLUTEN-FREE

ALSO BY KELLI AND PETER BRONSKI

No Gluten, No Problem Pizza
Artisanal Gluten-Free Cooking (Second Edition)
Gluten-Free Family Favorites
Artisanal Gluten-Free Cupcakes

ALSO BY PETER BRONSKI

The Gluten-Free Edge
(with Melissa McLean Jory, MNT)

KIDS COOK GLUTEN-FREE

OVER 65 FUN AND EASY RECIPES FOR YOUNG GLUTEN-FREE CHEFS

KELLI AND PETER BRONSKI

THE EXPERIMENT
NEW YORK

Kids Cook Gluten-Free: *Over 65 Fun and Easy Recipes for Young Gluten-Free Chefs*
All text, and photographs on pages 3, 16, 22, 30, 47, 53, 74, 75, 102, 103, 110 copyright © 2022 by Kelli and Peter Bronski
Cover photographs, and photographs on pages iv, vi, vii, viii, 4 (bottom right), 8 (bottom right), 11 (top left, bottom left), 12, 17, 18, 21, 23, 24, 25, 28, 29, 31, 35, 38, 42, 46, 49, 50, 52, 55, 58, 60, 63, 65, 66, 67, 68, 69, 72, 73, 76, 77, 78, 79, 80, 81, 82, 83, 84, 86, 88, 90, 91, 93, 94, 97, 101, 104, 106, 109, 112, 114 (bottom), 115 (bottom), 116, 117, 121, 123, 124, 125, 127, 128, 129, 130, 133, 134, 137, 139, 140, 141, 145, 146, 149, 150 copyright © 2022 by Emily Teater/The Luupe; Emily Teater and Madeline Tomseth/Set Creative Studios
Photographs on pages 2, 4, 5, 6, 7, 8, 9, 10, 11, 26, 33, 34, 39, 40, 41, 44, 45, 49 (top), 59, 61, 62, 64, 66 (top left), 85, 105, 107, 108, 113, 114 (top), 115 (top), 122, 124 (top), 125 (top) copyright © Adobe Stock

The Experiment, LLC
220 East 23rd Street, Suite 600
New York, NY 10010-4658
theexperimentpublishing.com

This book contains the opinions and ideas of its author. It is intended to provide helpful and informative material on the subjects addressed in the book. It is sold with the understanding that the author and publisher are not engaged in rendering medical, health, or any other kind of personal professional services in the book. The author and publisher specifically disclaim all responsibility for any liability, loss, or risk—personal or otherwise—that is incurred as a consequence, directly or indirectly, of the use and application of any of the contents of this book.

THE EXPERIMENT and its colophon are registered trademarks of The Experiment, LLC. Many of the designations used by manufacturers and sellers to distinguish their products are claimed as trademarks. Where those designations appear in this book and The Experiment was aware of a trademark claim, the designations have been capitalized.

The Experiment's books are available at special discounts when purchased in bulk for premiums and sales promotions as well as for fund-raising or educational use. For details, contact us at info@theexperimentpublishing.com.

Library of Congress Cataloging-in-Publication Data available upon request

ISBN 978-1-61519-855-9
Ebook ISBN 978-1-61519-856-6

Cover and text design by Beth Bugler

Manufactured in China

First printing July 2022
10 9 8 7 6 5 4 3 2 1

TO BOB AND LINDA TERRY: *Thank you for supporting my love of baking, allowing me to learn by doing in the kitchen, happily buying ingredients, and always helping with the dishes! I hope this book inspires future "little bakers"! Thanks, Mom and Dad!*

—Love, Kelli

TO THE SPIRIO CLAN, PAST AND PRESENT: *Thank you for fostering a family culture focused around cooking and enjoying delicious food together, in which the kids were not just welcomed but encouraged to help out in the kitchen. It continues with today's youngest generation.*

—Love, Pete

CONTENTS

SNACKS

SIDES

DINNER

DESSERT

READY ... SET ... COOK!

We hope this book inspires you to step into the kitchen and give cooking a try! We've filled these pages with recipes that are kid-tested and approved.

Take a look at this welcome section to learn common kitchen words, tools, and tips for how to be safe and make super tasty food.

Don't worry: Kitchens are made to get messy. Extra big messes can always be cleaned up. Mistakes can happen, especially when you're trying a new recipe for the first time. That's how you learn and have fun.

Remember: Cooking and baking with no gluten is no problem. You've got this. And it's going to look and—more important—taste great!

So, You're Gluten-Free!

There are lots of reasons to be gluten-free: celiac disease, gluten intolerance, or wheat allergy, to name just a few. Maybe you're not gluten-free, but you know someone who is, like a family member or friend. It doesn't matter, because this book is about one thing: how to make meals that are tasty, fun, and gluten-free. *Anyone* can enjoy these delicious recipes.

If you're new to cooking and eating gluten-free, here's a quick overview of some important things to keep in mind:

Sources of Gluten

Although we say the word "gluten" as if it's a single thing, it's actually a group of things. In particular, it's a family of proteins that comes from certain grains, including wheat, barley, rye, spelt, kamut, and einkorn. Avoid these grains, as well as foods made from these grains or their flours.

Certified GF Foods

Several organizations offer gluten-free certification; this is especially popular for packaged foods like chips, cereals, and breads. Look for a "certified gluten-free" logo or words. This can help give you the confidence that the ingredient or food you're buying is actually gluten-free.

Naturally GF Foods

Don't forget that there are also a *ton* of naturally gluten-free foods, including meats, fish, fresh fruits and vegetables, eggs, milk, butter—and the list goes on. Usually, these foods *won't* have a gluten-free certification. Don't worry. That's because they're almost always gluten-free already.

All fresh fruits and vegetables are naturally gluten-free!

LABEL READING

When you're gluten-free, it's important to *always* read the ingredients and allergen labels of the products you buy, to make sure they're GF. There are three places to check: 1) The actual list of ingredients (where you'll see ingredients like wheat or barley malt); 2) Any allergen statement (which will say something like CONTAINS: WHEAT); and 3) Any extra statements, like when foods that don't have a gluten-containing ingredient may have been processed on the same equipment as foods that do (in these cases, the label could say MAY CONTAIN: WHEAT or PROCESSED ON MACHINERY THAT ALSO PROCESSES WHEAT).

WATCH FOR HIDDEN GLUTEN

One reason it's important to always read labels is that gluten can hide in foods where we don't expect it. For example, most soy sauce—other than GF tamari soy sauce made from 100 percent soybeans—contains wheat. Similarly, oats themselves don't contain gluten, but they often get contaminated with gluten from wheat because of how they're grown and processed, so it's important to look for oats that are specifically labeled as gluten-free.

CROSS CONTACT

Cross contact refers to when gluten gets into foods where it doesn't belong. This can happen to packaged and prepared foods you buy at the supermarket when they are made. It can happen at restaurants. And if you're cooking in a kitchen where gluten-containing foods are also present, it can happen at home. If you share your kitchen between gluten-ous and gluten-free foods, make sure to always wash pots, pans, and utensils thoroughly before using them for gluten-free foods. Also wash the countertop, and your hands!

KITCHEN TERMS

Here are a few common words and techniques that come up often.

—BOIL—
To heat a liquid until it bubbles vigorously

—CHOP—
To cut with a knife into small uneven pieces

—DICE—
To cut with a knife into small square pieces

—GREASE—
To coat the inside of a pan or top of a baking sheet with oil or cooking spray

—MINCE—
To cut into very tiny pieces

—JUICE—
To squeeze the liquid (juice) out of citrus fruit (oranges, limes, and lemons)

—PINCH—
Amount of an ingredient you can pick up between your thumb and two fingers

-PULSE-
To use quick on-and-off motions to chop food in a food processor or blender

-PREP-
Short for prepare or preparation. Usually the first step in a recipe to help you get your kitchen and ingredients ready to go

-ROOM TEMPERATURE-
Neither hot nor cold, but about the temperature inside the kitchen. Usually refers to ingredients for baking, or how much to let something cool before you go on to the next step or serve it.

-SIMMER-
To heat liquid just until bubbles form at the edge of the pan, and keep it at that temperature. If it reaches a full boil, with bubbles floating up fast from the bottom of the pan, it's too hot, so lower the heat.

-SLICE-
To cut into thin strips or pieces

-STIR-
To use a spoon to mix and combine ingredients

-TOSS-
To gently mix ingredients by lifting and turning them over with a spatula, tongs, or your hands

-WHISK-
To vigorously mix ingredients with a whisk (see Utensils) until completely combined

-ZEST-
To use a Microplane grater or box grater to shave off tiny slivers of the colorful outer layer of citrus fruit (oranges, limes, and lemons). Always wash fruit with water before you zest it.

KITCHEN TOOLS

Here are some common kitchen items you'll use for cooking and baking.

APPLIANCES

BLENDER: A countertop electric appliance that mixes together and purees liquids and solids in a covered pitcher with a small spinning blade at the bottom; used to make smoothies and sauces

HANDHELD MIXER: A small handheld electric appliance with spinning beaters to mix ingredients together in a bowl; for mixing cake batter and beating egg whites

WAFFLE MAKER: A countertop electric appliance with two metal plates with many little indentations, connected by a hinge, that bakes batter in waffle shapes

COUNTERTOP GRIDDLE: A countertop electric appliance with a large, flat cooking surface; used to cook pancakes and quesadillas

IMMERSION BLENDER: A handheld electric appliance, also called a stick blender, with a small blade on the end that can be put into food to puree it and make it smooth; used for soups and sauces

FOOD PROCESSOR: A countertop electric appliance that quickly chops, cuts, or purees ingredients with a blade in an attached container; used to make salsa and hummus

STAND MIXER: A heavy countertop electric appliance with an attached mixing bowl, that mixes ingredients together with a paddle or whisk; used to make cookie dough and cake batter

MEASURING TOOLS

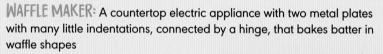

CANDY THERMOMETER: A cooking thermometer that can be attached to the side of a saucepan; the temperature display goes up to 400°F (200°C)

LIQUID MEASURING CUP: A clear glass or plastic cup with a spout and lines on the side; used to measure liquid ingredients

DIGITAL KITCHEN SCALE: A device used to measure the weight of food

MEASURING CUPS: Specifically sized metal or plastic cups (usually ¼ cup/60 ml, ⅓ cup/80 ml, ½ cup/120 ml, and 1 cup/240 ml); used to measure nonliquid ingredients

INSTANT-READ MEAT THERMOMETER: A thermometer with a sharp metal probe that you insert into food to take its internal temperature

MEASURING SPOONS: Specifically sized spoons (usually ¼ teaspoon, ½ teaspoon, 1 teaspoon, and 1 tablespoon); used to measure small amounts of ingredients

POTS AND PANS

BAKING DISH: An ovenproof glass or ceramic pan, often round, or oval, or rectangular

BAKING PANS: A square or rectangular metal pan with high sides, used for runny batters like cake and foods like lasagna. The most common sizes are 9-inch (23 cm) square and 9 x 13 inches (23 x 33 cm).

CAKE PAN: A round pan with high sides, typically used to bake cake batter. The most common sizes are 8-inch and 9-inch (20 and 23 cm).

COOKIE SHEET/BAKING SHEET: A large rectangular pan without raised edges, used to bake foods that cannot fall off the edge while baking, like cookies and pizza

MUFFIN PAN: A pan with 12 connected cups; used for muffins and cupcakes

NONSTICK SKILLET: A skillet with a special surface coating that helps prevent food from sticking to it; used for cooking eggs or frying fish. You usually need to use a plastic or rubber utensil (not metal) to avoid damaging the nonstick surface.

RIMMED BAKING SHEET: A large rectangular pan with a 1-inch (2.5 cm) raised edge that prevents any liquid from spilling in the oven, like when roasting vegetables

SAUCEPAN: A pot with a long, thin handle, usually deeper than it is wide; used for simmering and boiling. Comes in various sizes: small = 2 quarts (2 L), medium = 3 quarts (3 L), and large = 4½ quarts (4.3 L).

SKILLET: A round pan with a long handle, wide, flat bottom, and shallow sides; used for frying and cooking foods in small amounts of fat. Comes in various sizes: small = 8 inches (20 cm), medium = 10 inches (25 cm), and large = 12 inches (30 cm). Also sometimes called a frying pan.

UTENSILS

BASTING BRUSH: Used to brush small amounts of liquid onto the top of foods

BOX GRATER: A square metal box with different sized cutting holes on each side; used to shred cheese and zest citrus fruit

CAN OPENER: A device with a small, round blade used to open cans

CITRUS JUICER: A handheld tool that presses the juice from lemons, limes, and oranges; insert a piece of fruit into the juicer and squeeze the handles together

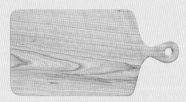

COLANDER: A large bowl, typically plastic or metal, with holes all over, on a raised base or feet; used to drain water out of food

CUTTING BOARD: A flat, durable piece of plastic or wood, used to hold food being cut

GARLIC PRESS: A handheld utensil used to squeeze garlic through tiny holes when you squeeze the handles together, so the garlic is cut finely or mashed without using a knife

KNIVES: Use a knife that's comfortable for your hand. If chopping something is too tricky, ask an adult for help. A small steak knife might be more comfortable at first. Then you can switch to a chef's knife when you feel confident about cutting safely.

① **Butter knife:** Small, with a rounded blade that isn't sharp

② **Chef's knife:** Large, general-purpose kitchen knife, usually 6 to 10 inches (15 to 25 cm) long, with a blade that curves upward along its length and ends in a narrow point; very sharp

③ **Palette knife:** A thin, flexible blade with a rounded tip, used to spread frosting; not sharp

④ **Paring knife:** A small, short blade; very sharp

⑤ **Serrated knife:** Has a wavy or scalloped edge; used to cut bread (also called a bread knife); very sharp

⑥ **Steak knife:** Small, with a sharp blade, usually used at the dinner table; the edge may be straight or serrated

Curl your fingers to keep them safe when using a knife.

LADLE: A long-handled utensil with a cup-shaped bowl at the end; used to scoop and pour liquid, like pancake batter or pasta water

PARCHMENT PAPER: Thin paper used to line a baking pan to prevent food from sticking to it. Also enables you to move wet dough from one surface to another.

SALAD SPINNER: A large covered bowl with a strainer basket inside; the basket spins to remove water from greens

VEGETABLE PEELER: A tool with a slotted blade connected to a handle that removes only the outermost layer of skin from a fruit or vegetable

MICROPLANE GRATER: A long, narrow blade with many small, sharp-edged holes; used to finely grate cheese and zest citrus fruit

PIZZA CUTTER: A round blade attached to a handle; used to cut pizza

SPATULA: A long-handled plastic or metal utensil with a wide, flat, rigid end; used to flip pancakes and burgers and remove food from a baking sheet

VEGETABLE SCRUB BRUSH: A firm-bristled, handheld brush used to clean dirt from vegetables

OVEN MITTS: Insulated mittens worn to protect your hands from hot pans and ingredients

RUBBER SPATULA: A utensil with a long handle and a wide, flexible end; used to scrape food out of a bowl and spread food in pans

TONGS: A two-part utensil used to grip and lift items

WHISK: A long-handled utensil ending in thin wire loops; used to mix ingredients together quickly

WIRE RACK: A tight metal grid, elevated on small feet to allow air circulation around the food placed on it

TIPS AND TRICKS

Follow this advice to stay safe and have fun while making this book's recipes.

1 Read the entire recipe before you start to make it, so you know what to expect.

2 Pull out all ingredients and tools that you need for the recipe.

3 Wash your hands before you begin making any recipe, and after you touch raw meat, fish, or separated eggs.

4 Never use a cutting board that was used for raw meat to cut foods that won't get cooked. If you have only a single cutting board, slice the raw meat last when prepping ingredients for a recipe. If you have two cutting boards, use one for raw meat and the other for fresh or uncooked foods.

5 Ask an adult for help if you need it. Your safety is the number one most important thing! Be very careful around the stovetop, oven, and boiling water.

6 Protect your hands and arms from heat and steam. You'll definitely use oven mitts to take hot pans out of the oven. But you may also want to use oven mitts for handling your pots, saucepans, and lids; their handles can get hot, and steam can burn your hands and arms—for example, when stirring boiling pasta or pouring cooked pasta and boiling water into a colander. Please keep yourself safe! If anything feels hot to touch, ask for help from an adult or wear oven mitts.

7 **MEASURE INGREDIENTS CAREFULLY.**

- If you have a digital kitchen scale, use it! It's faster and more accurate than measuring cups. Place a bowl on the scale and press the "tare" or "zero" button to set the weight to zero. Add the ingredient to the bowl until you reach the right number of ounces or grams, then add the measured ingredient to your main mixing bowl. Always measure ingredients by themselves so you can take some out if you go over the measurement.

- If you're using measuring cups, spoon the dry ingredient into the cup until it's full. Then use the back of a butter knife to scrape across the top to remove any extra.

- When you measure brown sugar, push it down tightly into the measuring cup or spoon. Then when the cup or spoon is full, scrape across the top to remove any extra, the way you do with flour. This is what a recipe means when it says "packed brown sugar."

- Use a liquid measuring cup for liquids. Place the cup on a flat surface and get down so the lines on it are at eye level to make sure the liquid is at the measure you want.

8 STEADY YOUR CUTTING BOARD: When you use a cutting board, put a kitchen towel under it. This will stop it from moving around as you slice and chop, so you'll be less likely to cut yourself.

9 REDUCE FOOD WASTE: If a recipe calls for a whole fruit or vegetable like a lemon or onion but you don't use all of it, place it in an airtight container and store it in the refrigerator to use in another dish. Cut citrus fruit will keep for 4 days and onions for up to 2 weeks.

10 WATCH FOR GLUTEN: Gluten can hide in ingredients like soy sauce. In the recipes, we specify "GF" before ingredients where you should pay extra special attention to the label.

11 USING AN ELECTRIC MIXER: Start slow, then increase the speed when the ingredients begin to come together. Otherwise, you can end up with liquids splashing out and flour flying in the air!

12 **MELTING BUTTER:** When a recipe calls for melted butter, cut the butter into pieces, put it in a microwave-safe bowl, cover it with a plate, and microwave it for 20 to 40 seconds, until it's completely melted. You may need to stir the butter a little to finish melting it. The bowl will be warm, so be careful when you take it out of the microwave. Or you can put the butter in a small saucepan and heat it on the stovetop over medium-low heat.

13 **PEELING GARLIC:** Lay the garlic clove on the cutting board and squish it with the side of the knife to break the clove

and split the skin, then remove the papery skin.

14 **ROOM TEMPERATURE BUTTER:** Room-temperature butter has been out of the refrigerator long enough so it's slightly soft when you touch it. (This typically takes about 1 hour.) If you need butter to get softer more quickly, unwrap it, slice it into pieces with a butter knife, and place it on a microwave-safe plate. Microwave it at 50 percent power for 10 to 15 seconds. Watch closely, because you don't want it to melt.

15 **SEPARATING EGGS:** Crack the egg into a small bowl and use your fingers to scoop out the yolk and put it in a different small bowl, being careful to not break it.

16 **TESTING PASTA TO SEE IF IT IS DONE:** Take one piece of pasta out of the water with a spoon and let it cool a little, then taste it. If it feels right to you, it's ready.

17 **WHISKING IN A SMALL CONTAINER:** In a liquid measuring cup or small bowl, hold the handle of the whisk straight up between the palms of your hands and rub them together to spin the whisk back and forth.

BRAND RECOMMENDATIONS

Some recipes call for using gluten-free ingredients, like sandwich bread or pasta, that you can buy from the store. You can choose from different brands of gluten-free food depending on what's available at your grocery store. But here are a few brands we know and love that will probably be easy to find.

BAGUETTE

Schär

CEREAL

Corn Chex

CRACKERS

Glutino crackers

Mary's Gone Crackers

RW Garcia sweet potato crackers

Blue Diamond Nut Thins

PASTA

Jovial

Tinkyáda

SANDWICH BREAD

Canyon Bakehouse

Rudi's

TAMARI GF SOY SAUCE

San-J

Eden Foods

ALL-PURPOSE FLOUR BLEND

King Arthur Gluten-Free Measure for Measure Flour

Note: Some of these brands make only gluten-free foods. But some companies make a variety of products—both gluten-free and gluten-full. Always read labels and make sure you're buying the gluten-free version.

If you have trouble finding the King Arthur all-purpose GF flour at your local market, or you're interested in making your own blend, try mixing up our signature Artisan Gluten-Free Flour Blend. We first developed this recipe more than 10 years ago, and it has remained a part of our gluten-free baking ever since!

ARTISAN GLUTEN-FREE FLOUR BLEND

PREP TIME: 5 minutes

INGREDIENTS

SINGLE BATCH
Makes about 3 cups (375 g)

1¼ cups (156 g) brown rice flour

¾ cup (88 g) sorghum flour

⅔ cup (90 g) cornstarch

¼ cup (37 g) potato starch

1 tablespoon plus 1 teaspoon (14 g) potato flour

1 teaspoon (3 g) xanthan gum

TOOLS

Digital kitchen scale or measuring cups

Measuring spoons, optional

Large bowl

Whisk

Airtight storage container

In the large bowl, whisk all the ingredients together thoroughly, breaking up any lumps. Store in an airtight container for up to 3 months in the pantry or 6 months in the refrigerator.

BREAKFAST

CHOCOLATE CHIP PANCAKES

MAKES: twelve 3-inch (7.5 cm) pancakes **PREP TIME:** 15 minutes **COOK TIME:** 15 minutes

Call 'em pancakes, flapjacks, or hotcakes. No matter what name you give them, they're an easy and delicious breakfast. This recipe makes them even better with the addition of mini chocolate chips. Serve with a drizzle of maple syrup or a dusting of confectioners' sugar. Yum!

INGREDIENTS

1 cup (125 g) GF all-purpose flour blend

1 tablespoon sugar

2 teaspoons baking powder

¼ teaspoon salt

1 cup (240 ml) milk

1 large egg

1 teaspoon GF pure vanilla extract

2 tablespoons unsalted butter, melted (see page 12)

GF nonstick cooking spray

¼ cup (45 g) mini chocolate chips

TOOLS

Digital kitchen scale or measuring cups

Measuring spoons

Medium bowl

Whisk

Electric countertop griddle or large skillet on the stovetop

Ladle or ¼-cup (60 ml) measuring cup

Spatula

MAKE THE BATTER

1 In the medium bowl, whisk together the flour, sugar, baking powder, and salt.

2 Add the milk, egg, and vanilla and whisk again.

3 Add the melted butter and whisk until the batter is smooth.

COOK THE PANCAKES

4 Heat the griddle to medium-high heat.

5 Grease the griddle with cooking spray.

6 Use the ladle or measuring cup to pour batter onto the hot griddle. Leave enough room between pancakes so their edges don't touch.

7 While they're still wet, sprinkle the top of each pancake with about 1 teaspoon of the chocolate chips.

CHEF TIP
Using a ladle makes it easy to pour the batter

8 When the surface of the pancakes is slightly puffed and the edges are dry, about 2 minutes, use the spatula to lift the edge of one pancake and peek at the bottom. If it's golden brown, it's ready to flip. Flip the pancakes and cook the other side until golden brown, 1 to 2 minutes.

9 Repeat with the remaining batter to make 12 pancakes. Serve warm.

BLUEBERRY PANCAKES:

Use 1 cup (140 g) blueberries (fresh or frozen) instead of the chocolate chips. Sprinkle 1 heaping tablespoon of the berries on each pancake.

17

HOMESTYLE WAFFLES

MAKES: eight 7-inch (18 cm) waffles   **PREP TIME:** 15 minutes   **COOK TIME:** 40 minutes (5 minutes per waffle)

Who doesn't love a hot waffle (or two!) for breakfast? With a waffle maker and this recipe, you can have them anytime. They're especially good fresh on weekend mornings, but you can save them in the freezer to enjoy later, like on a weekday before school. This recipe makes Eggo-style waffles, but the total number of waffles you can make will depend on the size of your waffle maker. Serve with your favorite waffle toppings like maple syrup, confectioners' sugar, or fresh fruit.

INGREDIENTS

GF nonstick cooking spray, optional

1¾ cups (218 g) GF all-purpose flour blend

1 tablespoon baking powder

½ teaspoon salt

2 large eggs

1¾ cups (420 ml) milk

1 teaspoon GF pure vanilla extract

8 tablespoons (1 stick) unsalted butter, melted (see page 12)

TOOLS

Digital kitchen scale or measuring cups

Measuring spoons

Waffle maker

Medium bowl

Whisk

Ladle or ½-cup (120 ml) measuring cup

Tongs

Wire rack

DO THE PREP

1 Heat the waffle maker. Most waffle makers are nonstick with a black finish on the inside. If that sounds like your waffle maker, continue to the next step. If the inside of your waffle maker is shiny metal, spray the two halves with cooking spray before you make each waffle.

MAKE THE BATTER

2 In the medium bowl, whisk together the flour, baking powder, and salt.

3 Add the eggs, milk, and vanilla and whisk again.

4 Add the melted butter and whisk until the batter is smooth.

COOK THE WAFFLES

5 Use the ladle or measuring cup to pour batter onto the bottom half of the hot waffle maker, until the batter reaches about 1 inch (2.5 cm) from the edge.

6 Close the lid and let the waffle cook, without peeking, until the indicator light on the waffle maker goes off or on (depending on what kind of waffle maker you have—read the instructions to check). The time will vary, but it typically takes about 5 minutes.

7 Open the waffle maker. The waffle should be golden brown when it's done. Use the tongs to remove the waffle and set it on the wire rack. (This will prevent the waffle from getting soggy and keep it crispy until you're ready to serve.)

8 Repeat, cooking waffles until all the batter is used up. Serve warm.

CRUMB CAKE

MAKES: 9 servings **PREP TIME:** 20 minutes **COOK TIME:** 25 to 30 minutes

Don't let this recipe's longer list of ingredients scare you away—it's as easy as throwing a bunch of stuff in a bowl and stirring! Plus, the moist cake and sweet streusel topping are *so* worth it. That's why crumb cake has become a super popular and delicious breakfast treat everywhere from New York City and Poland to Germany, where it's known as *streuselkuchen*.

INGREDIENTS

GF nonstick cooking spray

STREUSEL TOPPING

¾ cup (94 g) GF all-purpose flour blend

⅓ cup (76 g) packed brown sugar

1 teaspoon ground cinnamon

¼ teaspoon salt

6 tablespoons (¾ stick) unsalted butter, cold

CAKE BATTER

¾ cup (150 g) granulated sugar

6 tablespoons (¾ stick) unsalted butter, room temperature (see page 12)

1 teaspoon GF pure vanilla extract

1 large egg

1 large egg white (see page 12; discard the yolk)

½ cup (120 ml) milk

2 tablespoons sour cream

1½ cups (188 g) GF all-purpose flour blend

1¼ teaspoons baking powder

1 teaspoon xanthan gum

½ teaspoon baking soda

½ teaspoon salt

Confectioners' sugar

TOOLS

Digital kitchen scale or measuring cups

Measuring spoons

9-inch (23 cm) square baking pan

2 small bowls

Large spoon

Cutting board

Butter knife

Stand mixer or handheld mixer and medium bowl

Rubber spatula

DO THE PREP

1 Preheat the oven to 350°F (180°C).

2 Grease the baking pan with cooking spray.

MAKE THE STREUSEL TOPPING

3 In one of the small bowls, stir together the flour, brown sugar, cinnamon, and salt with the large spoon.

4 On the cutting board, use the butter knife to cut the butter into small pieces. (Smaller pieces will be easier to work into the flour mixture.)

5 Add the butter to the flour mixture. Use your fingers to pinch and squeeze the butter with the other ingredients until it's all mixed together and looks like small crumbles. Set the streusel aside.

MAKE THE CAKE BATTER

6 Add the granulated sugar and butter to the bowl of the stand mixer. Mix on medium speed until fluffy, about 2 minutes. (For a helpful picture, see Confetti Cupcakes, page 124.) Add the vanilla and mix again to combine.

7 Add the egg and egg white and mix until combined. Stop the mixer and scrape down the inside of the bowl with the rubber spatula so all the batter ends up at the bottom.

8 Add the milk and sour cream and mix again. (The batter will be very thin at this point.)

9 In the second small bowl, whisk together the flour, baking powder, xanthan gum, baking soda, and salt, breaking up any lumps.

10 Add the flour mixture to the wet ingredients. Mix on medium speed until thoroughly combined and smooth, about 15 seconds.

11 Use the rubber spatula to spread the batter in the prepared baking pan, scraping all the batter out of the bowl and smoothing the top.

12 Use your fingers to sprinkle the streusel topping evenly over the surface of the batter, breaking any large clumps into smaller pieces.

BAKE THE CAKE

13 Put the baking pan in the oven. Bake for 25 to 30 minutes, until a toothpick inserted in the center comes out almost clean. (A few small crumbs on the toothpick are OK.)

14 Wearing oven mitts, carefully remove the cake from the oven. Let it cool in the baking pan for 5 minutes. Then dust the top with confectioners' sugar. Use a butter knife to cut the cake into 9 squares.

15 Enjoy slightly warm or at room temperature. Cover any uneaten cake and store at room temperature for up to 3 days.

CHEF TIP
If the eggs are still cold from the refrigerator, soak them in a bowl of hot tap water for 10 minutes to warm them enough.

POPOVERS

MAKES: 12 popovers   **PREP TIME:** 15 minutes   **COOK TIME:** 30 minutes

This magical muffin is an American version of a Yorkshire pudding from England. (Although the British call it a "pudding," if you're in the United States you'd probably describe it as a roll.) One look and you'll see where they get their name: While baking, these eggy wonders inflate and pop up and over the top of the muffin pan! They're wonderful plain on their own, dusted with confectioners' sugar, or spread with your favorite jam.

INGREDIENTS

1 cup (240 ml) milk

1¼ cups (167 g) cornstarch

5 large eggs, room temperature

4 tablespoons (½ stick) unsalted butter, melted (see page 12)

1½ teaspoons GF pure vanilla extract

½ teaspoon salt

TOOLS

Digital kitchen scale or measuring cups

Measuring spoons

12-cup muffin pan or popover pan

Microwave-safe bowl or small saucepan

Large liquid measuring cup or medium bowl

Whisk

Oven mitts

Ladle or large spoon

DO THE PREP

1 Put the muffin pan in the oven, then preheat the oven to 425°F (220°C).

2 Put the milk in the microwave-safe bowl and microwave for about 1 minute until warm. Or heat it until warm in the small saucepan on the stovetop over medium heat.

MAKE THE BATTER

3 In the large measuring cup, whisk together the cornstarch and eggs until smooth. (If you don't have a large liquid measuring cup, that's OK. Just use a medium bowl and a ladle to spoon out the batter later.)

4 Add 1½ tablespoons of the butter, the vanilla, and the salt. Whisk to combine.

5 While whisking, add the warm milk. Whisk until fully mixed and smooth.

BAKE THE POPOVERS

6 Wearing oven mitts, carefully remove the hot pan from the oven. Quickly add ½ teaspoon of the remaining melted butter into each cup.

7 Carefully pour or ladle the batter into the hot cups. Each cup will be a little over half full.

8 Wearing oven mitts, put the filled pan in the oven. (Ask an adult to help you do this if you need to!)

9 Bake for 20 minutes, then turn the oven down to 350°F (180°C). Bake for 10 minutes more, until the popovers are golden brown. Don't open the oven until the end of the 10 minutes, or the popovers will collapse!

10 Wearing oven mitts, carefully remove the pan from the oven. Allow the popovers to cool in the pan for about 5 minutes. Then use a fork to remove them from the pan. If the popovers stick, use a knife to loosen them around the edge of the cups. Enjoy the popovers warm.

FRENCH TOAST SCONES

MAKES: 12 scones **PREP TIME:** 20 minutes **COOK TIME:** 15 minutes

The vanilla-and-cinnamon goodness of French toast packed into a warm,
freshly baked scone. What's not to love?

INGREDIENTS

1¾ cups (219 g) GF all-purpose flour blend

¼ cup (50 g) sugar

1 tablespoon baking powder

2 teaspoons ground cinnamon

1 teaspoon xanthan gum

½ teaspoon salt

6 tablespoons (¾ stick) unsalted butter, cold

½ cup (120 ml) heavy cream

1 large egg

2 teaspoons GF pure vanilla extract

Icing (page 120), optional

TOOLS

Digital kitchen scale or measuring cups	Cutting board
	Butter knife
	Small bowl
Measuring spoons	Rubber spatula
Medium bowl	Baking sheet
Large spoon	Oven mitts

DO THE PREP

1 Preheat the oven to 375°F (190°C).

MAKE THE DOUGH

2 In the medium bowl, stir together the flour, sugar, baking powder, cinnamon, xanthan gum, and salt with the spoon.

3 On the cutting board, use the butter knife to cut the butter into small pieces. (Smaller pieces will be easier to work into the flour.)

4 Add the butter to the flour mixture. Use your fingers to pinch and squeeze the butter with the flour until it's all mixed together and looks like small crumbles. (For a helpful picture, see Biscuits, page 103.)

5 Add the cream, egg, and vanilla to a small bowl and whisk to combine.

6 Add the cream mixture to the flour mixture, and stir with the spoon to form a rough dough. Finish mixing it with your hands until it's completely combined and smooth.

SHAPE THE DOUGH

7 Clean the counter. Use the rubber spatula to scrape the dough onto the counter.

8 With your hands, shape the dough into a log about 12 inches (30 cm) long. Flatten it to 3 inches (8 cm) wide.

9 Cut the log in half and then cut each half into 3 equal rectangles. Cut each rectangle along the diagonal to make 12 triangles.

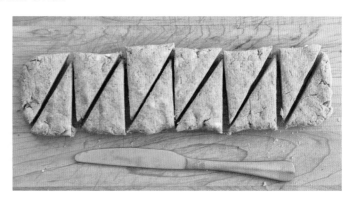

BAKE AND ENJOY

10 Separate the scones and place them about 2 inches (5 cm) apart on the baking sheet.

11 Put the baking sheet in the oven. Bake for 12 to 15 minutes, until the edges are light golden brown.

12 Wearing oven mitts, carefully remove the baking sheet from the oven.

13 Allow the scones to cool on the baking sheet for a few minutes before serving. Serve warm or at room temperature.

EGGSCELLENT EGGS

EACH STYLE MAKES 1 SERVING

Eggs are packed with protein (yay, strong muscles!) and can be eaten all kinds of different ways. This recipe gives you the option to prepare them in three popular styles—scrambled, over-easy, or hard-boiled.

SCRAMBLED

PREP TIME: 5 minutes   **COOK TIME:** about 5 minutes

INGREDIENTS

2 large eggs

1 tablespoon milk

⅛ teaspoon (generous pinch) salt

⅛ teaspoon (generous pinch) black pepper

1 tablespoon olive oil or unsalted butter

TOOLS

Measuring spoons

Small bowl

Whisk

Small nonstick skillet

Rubber spatula

DO THE PREP

1 Crack the eggs into the bowl. Add the milk, salt, and pepper.

2 Use the whisk or fork to break up the egg yolks and mix until everything is a consistent yellow color.

COOK THE EGGS

3 Heat the skillet on the stovetop over medium-high heat for about 2 minutes. When the skillet is hot, add the oil or butter. Swirl the skillet to coat the bottom evenly.

4 Carefully pour the egg mixture into the skillet and leave it until it starts to bubble, less than a minute.

5 Use the spatula to stir the eggs. Then tilt the skillet to let some of the runny eggs move to the bottom so they can cook, too.

6 Let the eggs cook until they are nearly dry, about 2 minutes more. Flip them over to finish cooking on top, about 1 more minute.

7 Use the spatula to move the eggs to a plate. Serve hot!

OVER-EASY

PREP TIME: 5 minutes   COOK TIME: about 5 minutes

INGREDIENTS

2 large eggs

GF nonstick cooking spray

⅛ teaspoon (generous pinch) salt

⅛ teaspoon (generous pinch) black pepper

TOOLS

Measuring spoons

Small nonstick skillet

Small bowl

Spatula

DO THE PREP

1 Heat the skillet on the stovetop over medium-high heat for about 2 minutes.

2 Crack 1 of the eggs into the bowl.

3 When the skillet is hot, coat the inside with cooking spray.

COOK THE EGGS

4 Carefully pour the egg into the skillet. Quickly crack the second egg into the bowl and pour it into the skillet, leaving space between the two eggs. (If the eggs touch, it's not a problem—just use the spatula to cut between the whites.)

5 Sprinkle the top of each egg with salt and pepper.

6 When the egg whites are set and solid white all the way around the yolk, after about 2 minutes, use the spatula to flip the eggs, one at a time. Be gentle so you don't break the yolks!

7 Cook for about 1 minute on the second side for runny yolks. Cook for 2 minutes if you'd like the yolks more cooked.

8 Use the spatula to carefully move the eggs to a plate. Serve hot!

HARD-BOILED

PREP TIME: 5 minutes   COOK TIME: 12 minutes

INGREDIENTS

2 large eggs

Cold water

Ice cubes

Salt and black pepper, optional

TOOLS

Small saucepan with lid

Colander

COOK THE EGGS

1 Place the eggs in the saucepan and add enough cold water so there's 1 inch (2.5 cm) of water above the eggs.

2 Put the saucepan on the stovetop over high heat and bring the water and eggs to a boil. Boil for 1 minute.

3 Turn off the heat, move the saucepan to a cool burner, and cover it with its lid. Leave it to sit for 12 minutes.

4 Place the colander in the sink. Remove the lid and carefully pour the water and cooked eggs into the colander to drain.

5 Refill the same pot with very cold water and add a few ice cubes. Put the eggs in the cold water and leave them until they are completely cooled, about 10 minutes.

6 Enjoy the eggs immediately or refrigerate them in an airtight container until you're ready to eat them, up to 1 week. To peel, gently tap each egg on the counter on all sides until the shell is cracked all over, then peel off the pieces of shell. If the shell sticks, peel the egg under cold water. The eggs are delicious seasoned with a little sprinkle of salt and pepper.

AVOCADO TOAST

MAKES: 2 servings **PREP TIME:** 10 minutes

Avocados are originally from Mexico. We call them a "superfood" because they're full of lots of things that are super good for you: vitamins, minerals, and healthy fats. And they're the hero of this easy, tasty recipe, in which salt and lime juice work together to brighten the creamy mashed avocado on top of delightfully toasty bread. We're licking our lips already!

INGREDIENTS

2 slices GF sandwich bread

1 ripe avocado

½ lime (about 1 tablespoon juice)

¼ teaspoon salt

TOOLS

Measuring spoons

Chef's knife
(see Knives, page 8)

Large spoon

Small bowl

Citrus juicer

Fork

DO THE PREP

1 Use a toaster or the oven to toast the slices of bread until they're as brown and crispy as you like.

2 Avocados have a large, hard pit in the center. Here's how to cut the avocado and remove the pit:

❶ Use the chef's knife to carefully slice the avocado lengthwise through the center until the knife reaches the hard pit.

❷ Leaving the knife blade touching the pit, rotate the avocado in a straight circle. Go all the way around until you return to your original cut. Remove the knife.

❸ Hold the avocado with both hands and twist the sides in opposite directions to open it.

❹ Use the large spoon to remove the pit. Then scoop the avocado flesh out of the peel and put the flesh in the small bowl.

EGGSCELLENT AVOCADO TOAST:

Add an egg over-easy (see page 27) to each slice of avocado toast to turn this into a more filling breakfast or lunch.

3 Put the lime half in the citrus juicer and squeeze out the juice on top of the avocado. (If you don't have a citrus juicer, you can squeeze the lime, cut side down, with your hand until the juice comes out.) Add the salt.

4 Use the fork to mash the avocado until it's smooth.

ASSEMBLE AND ENJOY

5 Use the fork to spread the mashed avocado evenly on each slice of toast.

6 Avocados will start to turn brown when exposed to the air, so serve right away.

MINI QUICHES

MAKES: 12 quiches   **PREP TIME:** 30 minutes   **COOK TIME:** 40 minutes

A quiche is a French tart with a pastry crust shell, a soft and eggy custard, and a cheese, meat, and/or veggie filling. Although they sound fancy, they're pretty easy to make—and delicious! Traditionally, you would make a single large quiche in a pie plate. But by using a muffin pan, you can make a dozen cute, personal mini quiches. Enjoy one or two for a light breakfast, serve a few more as part of a larger meal, or add a salad for "breakfast for dinner."

INGREDIENTS

GF nonstick cooking spray

FILLINGS AND CUSTARD

4 pieces thin-sliced deli ham

2 green onions

½ cup (120 ml) milk

¼ cup (60 ml) heavy cream

3 large eggs

¼ teaspoon salt

¼ teaspoon black pepper

½ cup (56 g) shredded cheddar

CRUST

1⅓ cups (167 g) GF all-purpose flour blend

½ teaspoon salt

4 tablespoons (½ stick) unsalted butter, cold

¼ cup (60 ml) cold water

1 large egg

1 teaspoon apple cider vinegar

TOOLS

Digital kitchen scale or measuring cups

Measuring spoons

Muffin pan

Cutting board

Chef's knife (see Knives, page 8)

3 small bowls

Medium bowl

Butter knife

Whisk

Large spoon

Ladle

Oven mitts

MAKE IT YOUR OWN:

This recipe uses ham, green onions, and cheddar cheese, but you can substitute any combo of fillings that you like. Try bacon, bell peppers, and caramelized onions—or just the custard with no fillings at all.

DO THE PREP

1 Preheat the oven to 350°F (180°C).

2 Grease the inside of the muffin pan cups with cooking spray.

3 On the cutting board, use the chef's knife to cut the ham into small pieces. Set it aside in one of the small bowls.

4 Rinse and dry the green onions. Lay them on the cutting board and use the chef's knife to cut off the root ends and slice the green onions into thin coins. Set them aside in a second small bowl.

MAKE THE CRUST

5 In the medium bowl, mix together the flour and salt with the spoon.

6 On the cutting board, use a butter knife to cut the butter into small pieces. (Smaller pieces will be easier to work into the flour mixture.)

7 Add the butter to the flour. Use your fingers to pinch and squeeze until it's all mixed together and looks like small crumbles. (For a helpful picture, see Biscuits, page 103.)

8 Whisk together the cold water, egg, and vinegar in the third small bowl.

9 Add the egg mixture to the flour mixture and stir with the spoon to form a smooth dough.

10 Place the dough onto the counter and roll it into a "snake" about 12 inches (30 cm) long. Cut the snake into twelve 1-inch (2.5 cm) pieces: Start by cutting the snake in half, then cut each half in half, then cut each quarter into three pieces.

11 Place one piece of dough in each cup of the prepared muffin pan. Use your fingers to press the dough across the bottom and up the sides of each muffin cup.

MAKE THE CUSTARD

12 Add the milk, cream, eggs, salt, and pepper to the medium bowl you used to make the dough. Whisk until everything is completely combined and a consistent light-yellow color.

ASSEMBLE AND BAKE

13 Divide the ham and green onion equally among the pastry shells in the muffin cups. Top with the cheese. Ladle the custard over the fillings until it just reaches the top edge of the pastry shell in each cup.

14 Put the filled pan in the oven. Bake the quiches for 40 minutes, until the custard is slightly puffed and golden brown.

15 Wearing oven mitts, carefully remove the muffin pan from the oven. Allow the quiches to cool in the pan for about 10 minutes.

16 Use the tip of the butter knife to pop each quiche out of the pan. Serve warm.

17 Store any uneaten quiches in the refrigerator in an airtight container for up to 1 week. You can reheat them in the microwave when the craving strikes.

31

BACON AND SAUSAGE

MAKES: 6 to 7 servings (about 2 pieces per serving)

Sometimes you might crave a sweet breakfast. But other times, a savory and salty breakfast is just what your taste buds need. A side of bacon or sausage along with eggs, pancakes, or waffles can be the perfect way to start your day. Here are multiple ways to prepare them: the oven-baked option is great when you want to cook many pieces at a time; the stovetop or microwave options cook fewer pieces at a time, so you'll need to cook in batches. Choose what works best for you and your family. And remember to be careful when cooking the stovetop version, because the fat will pop and splatter.

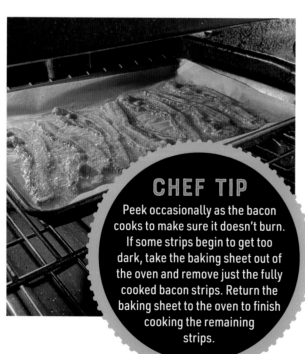

CHEF TIP

Peek occasionally as the bacon cooks to make sure it doesn't burn. If some strips begin to get too dark, take the baking sheet out of the oven and remove just the fully cooked bacon strips. Return the baking sheet to the oven to finish cooking the remaining strips.

BACON

INGREDIENTS

One 12- to 16-ounce (340 to 454 g) package bacon

OVEN-BAKED

PREP TIME: 5 minutes **COOK TIME:** 20 minutes

DO THE PREP

1 Preheat the oven to 400°F (200°C).

2 Tear off a piece of parchment paper the size of the rimmed baking sheet and line the baking sheet with it (put the paper on top). Line the plate with the paper towels.

TOOLS

Parchment paper

1 or 2 rimmed baking sheets

Large plate

Paper towels

Oven mitts

Tongs

COOK THE BACON

3 Lay the bacon strips on the parchment paper without overlapping them. (Use a second baking sheet if there are too many strips to fit on just one.) Wash your hands!

4 Put the baking sheet in the oven and bake for 14 to 17 minutes, until the bacon is brown and crispy (see Tip). Bake one sheet at a time if you're using more than one.

5 Wearing oven mitts, carefully remove the baking sheet from the oven. Be *very* careful not to touch the baking sheet with your bare hands—the pan and bacon drippings are very hot! Ask for help if you need to.

6 Use the tongs to take the crispy bacon off the baking sheet and set it on the prepared plate. Allow the bacon to cool for a minute, then remove the paper towel and serve warm.

STOVETOP

PREP TIME: 5 minutes **COOK TIME:** 20 minutes per batch

DO THE PREP

1 Line the plate with the paper towels.

TOOLS

Large plate
Paper towels
Large skillet
Tongs

COOK THE BACON

2 Place as many bacon strips as will fit without overlapping in a large skillet. Wash your hands!

3 Put the skillet with the bacon on the stovetop over medium-high heat.

4 Cook the bacon on one side until it starts to curl up at the edges, about 6 minutes. Use the tongs to flip the bacon. Let it cook on the second side until brown and crispy, about 2 minutes more.

5 Place the crispy bacon on the prepared plate. Allow the bacon to cool for a minute, then remove the paper towel and serve warm.

6 Repeat steps 3 through 5 with any remaining bacon strips.

MICROWAVE

PREP TIME: 5 minutes
COOK TIME: 5 minutes per batch

DO THE PREP

1 Line the microwave-safe plate with paper towels. Place 4 or 5 bacon strips on the plate without overlapping. Wash your hands!

TOOLS

Microwave-safe plate
Paper towels
Oven mitts
Tongs
Serving plate

COOK THE BACON

2 Cover the bacon with another paper towel. Microwave on high power for 3 minutes.

3 Check if the bacon is crispy. If it's not crispy enough, microwave for 1 minute more.

4 Take the plate out of the microwave. Be careful—even a microwave-safe plate can get hot. If it is hot, wear oven mitts to take it out. Use the tongs to transfer the cooked bacon to the serving plate.

5 Repeat steps 1 through 4 with the remaining bacon strips.

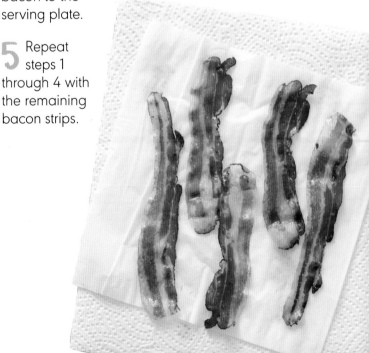

SAUSAGE

INGREDIENTS

One 12- to 16-ounce (340 to 454 g) package breakfast sausage links

1 tablespoon olive oil (stovetop version only)

OVEN-BAKED

PREP TIME: 5 minutes   COOK TIME: 18 to 22 minutes

DO THE PREP

1 Preheat the oven to 375°F (190°C).

2 Line the plate with paper towels.

COOK THE SAUSAGE

3 Place the sausage links in the baking pan in a single layer. Wash your hands!

4 Put the baking pan in the oven. Bake for 18 to 22 minutes, until the sausage is golden brown and cooked through. (When you cut a sausage open, it should be completely brown inside, with no pink).

5 Wearing oven mitts, carefully remove the baking pan from the oven. Use the tongs to transfer the cooked sausage to the prepared plate. Remove the paper towels when you're ready to serve.

TOOLS

Serving plate

Paper towels

9-inch (23 cm) square or 9 x 13-inch (23 x 33 cm) baking pan

Oven mitts

Tongs

STOVETOP

PREP TIME: 5 minutes   COOK TIME: 20 minutes

DO THE PREP

1 Heat the skillet on the stovetop over medium heat for about 2 minutes.

2 Line the plate with the paper towel.

TOOLS

Large skillet

Measuring spoons

Serving plate

Paper towels

Tongs

COOK THE SAUSAGE

3 Add the oil to the skillet, then carefully place the sausages in the skillet in a single layer. Wash your hands!

4 Cook the sausages uncovered, turning them over occasionally with the tongs, until browned and cooked through, about 15 minutes. (When you cut a sausage open, it should be completely brown inside, with no pink.)

5 Use the tongs to transfer the cooked sausages to the prepared plate. Remove the paper towel before serving.

NOTE: Pour any cooled bacon or sausage drippings into the garbage. *Do not* pour them down the sink drain! Compost or throw away any parchment paper or paper towels.

BREAKFAST BAKE

MAKES: 6 servings   **PREP TIME:** 20 minutes, plus 2 hours to overnight resting time   **COOK TIME:** 30 to 35 minutes

A "sausage, egg, and cheese" is a popular breakfast sandwich. This breakfast bake recipe gives you that same great combination of flavors, but it's made in the oven and easy to share. You can do steps 1 through 8 the night before, keep it in the refrigerator overnight, and bake it in the morning for a quick, easy breakfast.

DO THE PREP

1 Grease the baking pan with cooking spray.

2 Heat the skillet on the stovetop over medium-high heat.

3 Add the sausage to the skillet and use the spatula to break it into little pieces. Cook the sausage, stirring it a few times, until it is all browned and cooked through, about 10 minutes. Turn off the heat, move the skillet to a cool burner, and set it aside to cool while you finish the prep.

4 In the medium bowl, whisk the eggs, milk, and salt together until completely mixed and a consistent light-yellow color. Set aside.

5 On the cutting board, use a serrated knife to cut the bread into small cubes (about ½ inch/13 mm). Spread them across the bottom of the prepared baking pan.

6 Use the spatula to spread the cooked sausage over the bread cubes. Sprinkle the shredded cheese on top. Pour the egg mixture over everything.

7 Cover the baking pan and refrigerate it for at least 2 hours, or at most overnight, to give the bread time to soak in all the flavors.

COOK THE BREAKFAST BAKE

8 Preheat the oven to 350°F (180°C).

9 Uncover the baking pan and bake for 30 to 35 minutes, until the top has golden brown spots and the bake jiggles only a little when you move the baking pan.

10 Wearing oven mitts, remove the baking pan from the oven. Allow the bake to cool for a few minutes, then serve warm. Cover and refrigerate any uneaten bake for up to 1 week.

INGREDIENTS

- GF nonstick cooking spray
- 8 ounces (227 g) pork sausage meat, without casing
- 4 large eggs
- 1¼ cups (300 ml) milk
- ½ teaspoon salt
- 3 slices GF sandwich bread
- ½ cup (56 g) shredded sharp cheddar or mozzarella

TOOLS

Digital kitchen scale or measuring cups

Measuring spoons

9-inch (23 cm) square baking pan

Large skillet

Spatula

Medium bowl

Cutting board

Serrated knife

Oven mitts

LUNCH

NACHOS

MAKES: 4 servings   **PREP TIME:** 10 minutes   **COOK TIME:** 1 to 2 minutes

Whether you want a big plate all to yourself or a snack to share with family or friends, nachos are awesome. And because tortilla chips are usually made from 100 percent corn, they're naturally gluten-free, too! Customize them with your favorite combination of toppings—how about black beans and cilantro leaves?

INGREDIENTS

2 big handfuls (4 cups/100 g) GF tortilla chips

1 cup (112 g) shredded Mexican cheese blend or queso quesadilla

½ cup (115 g) salsa (see page 62 or 63)

2 tablespoons sour cream

1 tablespoon milk

TOPPINGS (OPTIONAL)

Guacamole (page 64)

Canned black beans, drained and rinsed

Canned pinto beans, drained and rinsed

Cooked taco meat (see page 94)

Sliced jalapeño chile

Cilantro leaves

TOOLS

Digital kitchen scale or measuring cups

Measuring spoons

Baking sheet

Oven mitts

Spoon

Small bowl

DO THE PREP

1 Move an oven rack to the middle position in the oven. Turn on the oven to broil.

ASSEMBLE THE INGREDIENTS

2 Spread the tortilla chips on the baking sheet in a single layer. Sprinkle evenly with the cheese.

3 Put the baking sheet in the oven and broil until the cheese is melted, about 1 minute. Watch while the cheese is melting to make sure the chips don't burn.

4 Wearing oven mitts, carefully remove the baking sheet from the oven.

FINISH AND SERVE

5 Being careful to not touch the hot baking sheet, spoon the salsa over the melted cheese.

6 In the small bowl, use a spoon to mix the sour cream and milk. Drizzle the mixture over the salsa. Add any toppings you like. Serve right away!

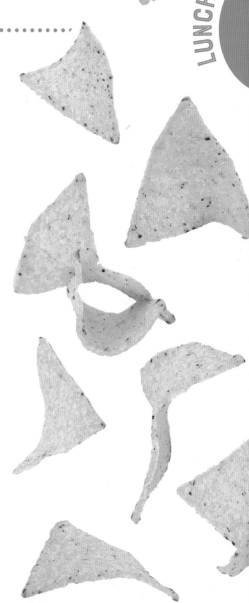

39

BLACK BEAN QUESADILLAS

MAKES: 4 quesadillas   **PREP TIME:** 15 minutes   **COOK TIME:** 20 minutes (about 5 minutes per quesadilla)

Quesadillas are a Mexican dish that starts with melted cheese inside a heated tortilla. But you can add lots of other fillings to make it even tastier. These quesadillas get a punch of extra flavor from taco-seasoned black beans. They're great with 5-Minute Tomato Salsa (page 62), Guacamole (page 64), and sour cream. If you have any leftover bean filling, you can freeze it in an airtight container to save for another day.

INGREDIENTS

- One 15-ounce (425 g) can black beans
- ½ lime (about 1 tablespoon juice)
- 1 teaspoon ground cumin
- ½ teaspoon garlic powder
- ¼ teaspoon salt
- ¼ teaspoon black pepper
- 1 cup (112 g) shredded queso quesadilla, Monterey Jack, or Mexican cheese blend
- 8 GF corn tortillas
- 1 tablespoon plus 1 teaspoon olive oil

TOOLS

Can opener	Citrus squeezer
Measuring spoons	Spoon
	Skillet
Digital kitchen scale or measuring cups	Spatula
	Cutting board
Colander	Chef's knife or pizza cutter (see Knives, page 8)
Food processor or medium bowl and potato masher	

DO THE PREP

1 Place the colander in the sink. Use the can opener to open the can of beans. Pour them into the colander and rinse with cold water. Pour the beans into the food processor (or medium bowl if you're not using a food processor).

2 Put the lime half in the citrus juicer and squeeze out the juice on top of the beans. (If you don't have a citrus juicer, you can use your hand to squeeze the lime, cut side down, until the juice comes out.)

3 Add the cumin, garlic powder, salt, and pepper to the beans. Blend until smooth (or mash with the potato masher to make the beans as smooth as you can).

ASSEMBLE THE QUESADILLAS

4 Lay out 4 corn tortillas. Use the spoon to spread about 2 tablespoons of the black bean mixture evenly on top of each tortilla. Sprinkle each with about ¼ cup (28 g) of the cheese. Top each with a second corn tortilla.

COOK THE QUESADILLAS

5 Heat the skillet on the stovetop over medium-high heat for 1 to 2 minutes, until a drop of water sizzles when you drop it on the skillet (see page 117).

Add about 1 teaspoon oil to the hot skillet. Using the spatula, carefully place one quesadilla in the skillet.

6 Cook until the bottom tortilla has golden brown spots, 1 to 2 minutes. (You can peek by lifting up the edge of the quesadilla with the spatula.)

7 Flip the quesadilla and cook until the cheese is melted and the second side also has golden spots, 1 to 2 minutes more.

SLICE AND ENJOY

8 Using the spatula, remove the quesadilla from the skillet and place it on the cutting board to cool for a minute. Then cut it into quarters using the chef's knife or pizza cutter.

9 Repeat steps 5 through 8 to make and cut the remaining quesadillas. Serve their cheesy goodness while they're warm.

BAKED MAC AND CHEESE

MAKES: 4 servings **PREP TIME:** 20 minutes **COOK TIME:** 20 to 25 minutes

Box mixes for gluten-free mac and cheese are fairly easy to find at the supermarket these days, but almost all of them use a packet of powdered cheese. This recipe lets you elevate your mac and cheese game with your pasta of choice and a cheese blend that'll knock your socks off. You can also serve the creamy mac and cheese without baking it, if you like!

INGREDIENTS

GF nonstick cooking spray

2 quarts (2 L) water

2 teaspoons salt

2 cups (224 g) GF short macaroni pasta (such as elbows or shells)

4 tablespoons (½ stick) unsalted butter

2 tablespoons GF all-purpose flour blend

1 cup (240 ml) milk

¼ teaspoon salt

¼ teaspoon black pepper

2 cups (224 g) shredded sharp cheddar

¼ cup (20 g) grated Parmesan

TOOLS

Measuring spoons

Digital kitchen scale or measuring cups

2-quart (2 L) baking dish or 9-inch (23 cm) square baking pan

Colander

Large saucepan

Large spoon

Medium saucepan

Whisk

Oven mitts

DO THE PREP

1 Preheat the oven to 350°F (180°C).

2 Grease the inside of the baking dish or baking pan with cooking spray.

3 Place a colander in the sink.

COOK THE MACARONI AND MAKE THE CHEESE SAUCE

4 Add the water and salt to a large saucepan, then bring to a boil on the stovetop over high heat.

5 Add the macaroni to the boiling water, turn the heat down to medium-high, and boil until it's al dente (see Tip). Stir the macaroni every few minutes to prevent it from sticking together.

6 While the macaroni is boiling, melt the butter in the medium saucepan on the stovetop over medium heat. When the butter is melted, add the flour and whisk until smooth. Cook for 1 minute, whisking constantly. (This will make a "roux," which is butter and flour cooked together and used to thicken a sauce.)

7 Add the milk, salt, and pepper to the roux and whisk until smooth. Cook, whisking occasionally, until the sauce thickens, about 5 minutes. Add the cheddar and whisk until it's melted and smooth, about 2 minutes. Turn off the heat and move the saucepan to a cool burner.

8 When the macaroni is al dente, carefully pour the water and cooked macaroni into the colander to drain. Add the drained macaroni back to the empty saucepan.

ASSEMBLE, BAKE, AND ENJOY

9 Pour the cheese sauce over the macaroni and stir to coat. Pour everything into the prepared baking dish. Sprinkle the Parmesan on top.

10 Put the baking dish in the oven and bake it for 20 to 25 minutes, until the top is golden brown.

11 Wearing oven mitts, remove the baking dish from the oven and allow it to cool for a few minutes before serving.

CHEF TIP

"Al dente" means that pasta is cooked through and soft but still a little chewy. To test if your pasta is done, take one piece out of the water with a spoon and let it cool a little, then taste it. If it feels right to you, it's ready. The amount of time will vary depending on the brand and type of pasta. Check the packaging for recommended cooking time.

GARLIC NOODLES

MAKES: 4 servings **PREP TIME:** 10 minutes **COOK TIME:** 20 minutes

If you're looking for a recipe that combines a short list of ingredients, fast and easy preparation, and tasty flavors—this is it! Plus, garlic is great for scaring away vampires and zombies. Sure, they're only pretend monsters. But it doesn't hurt to be extra safe!

INGREDIENTS

2 quarts (2 L) water

2 teaspoons salt

3 garlic cloves

2 cups (224 g) GF short macaroni pasta (such as penne, farfalle, or fusilli)

¼ cup (60 ml) olive oil

¼ teaspoon red pepper flakes, optional

Pinch each of salt and black pepper, optional

TOOLS

Measuring spoons

Digital kitchen scale or measuring cups

Large saucepan

Colander

Garlic press or cutting board and chef's knife

Small bowl

Large spoon

Large skillet

Ladle

Tongs

DO THE PREP

1 Add the water and 2 teaspoons salt to the saucepan, then bring it to a boil on the stovetop over high heat.

2 Place a colander in the sink.

3 Peel the papery skin off the garlic cloves (see page 12).

4 Squeeze the garlic through a garlic press into the small bowl. (If you don't have a garlic press, mince the garlic using the chef's knife and cutting board and scrape the garlic into the small bowl.)

COOK THE NOODLES AND MAKE THE GARLIC SAUCE

5 Add the noodles to the boiling water, then turn the heat down to medium-high. Boil until the noodles are al dente (see Baked Mac and Cheese, page 43). Stir the noodles every few minutes to prevent them from sticking together.

6 While the noodles are boiling, heat the skillet on the stovetop over medium heat for 1 to 2 minutes, until a drop of water sizzles when you drop it on the hot skillet (see page 117). Add the oil, garlic, and the red pepper flakes, if you're using them. Stir and cook about 2 minutes, until the garlic is very fragrant and starting to turn slightly golden. (If the garlic is turning dark brown, immediately remove the skillet from the heat because the garlic will become bitter if it burns.) Turn off the heat, move the skillet to a cool burner, and set it aside until the noodles are done.

7 When the cooking time for the noodles is almost up, use the ladle to add ¼ cup (60 ml) of the starchy cooking water to the oil and garlic; stir to combine.

8 When the cooking time is finished, carefully pour the water and cooked noodles into the colander to drain.

FINISH THE DISH AND ENJOY

9 Add the drained noodles to the garlic sauce and toss with the tongs to coat. Taste and add a pinch of salt and pepper, if you like. Serve hot.

PARMESAN AND BUTTER NOODLES

MAKES: 4 servings   PREP TIME: 10 minutes   COOK TIME: 20 minutes

Just because a recipe is simple doesn't mean it can't be delicious. These noodles are proof.
Just four ingredients! The Parmesan cheese adds a pleasant saltiness, while the butter
makes these noodles satisfyingly rich.

DO THE PREP

1 Add the water and salt to the saucepan, then bring it to a boil on the stovetop over high heat.

2 Place the colander in the sink.

COOK THE NOODLES AND START THE SAUCE

3 Add the noodles to the boiling water, turn the heat down to medium-high, and boil until the noodles are al dente (see Baked Mac and Cheese, page 43). Stir the noodles every few minutes to prevent them from sticking together.

4 Add the butter to the skillet on the stovetop over low heat. When the cooking time for the noodles is almost up, use the ladle to add ¼ cup (60 ml) of the starchy cooking water to the melted butter. Turn off the heat and move the skillet to a cool burner.

5 Carefully pour the water and cooked noodles into the colander to drain.

FINISH THE DISH AND ENJOY

6 Add the drained noodles and Parmesan to the butter mixture in the skillet. Toss with the tongs until the sauce is creamy and the noodles are coated evenly. Serve hot.

INGREDIENTS

- 2 quarts (2 L) water
- 2 teaspoons salt
- 2 cups (224 g) GF short macaroni pasta (such as penne, farfalle, or fusilli)
- 4 tablespoons (½ stick) unsalted butter
- ½ cup (40 g) grated Parmesan

TOOLS

Measuring spoons	Colander
Digital kitchen scale or measuring cups	Large skillet
	Ladle
	Oven mitts
	Tongs
Large saucepan	

MAKE IT YOUR OWN:

This recipe adds green onions, but add any combo of toppings that you like. Try shredded carrot, sliced mushrooms, sliced cooked chicken, or a hard-boiled egg (see page 27).

RAMEN

MAKES: 4 servings   **PREP TIME:** 5 minutes   **COOK TIME:** 15 minutes

Many Japanese-inspired dishes are known for their umami, a satisfying savoriness that's often described as the fifth flavor (alongside salty, sweet, bitter, and sour). These ramen noodles fit the bill, with slurp-worthy flavors that'll have you coming back for a second bowl.

INGREDIENTS

2 green onions (scallions)

4 cups (946 ml) GF chicken stock or broth, or vegetable stock to make this vegetarian

2 tablespoons GF tamari soy sauce

1 tablespoon honey

2 teaspoons sesame oil

1 to 2 teaspoons ground fresh chili paste (also called sambal oelek)

10 ounces (284 g) GF ramen noodles or rice noodles (see Tip)

TOOLS

Measuring spoons

Digital kitchen scale or measuring cups

Cutting board

Chef's knife (see Knives, page 8)

Large saucepan

Large spoon

DO THE PREP

1 Rinse and dry the green onions. Lay them on the cutting board and use the chef's knife to cut off the root ends and slice the green onions into thin coins.

COOK THE NOODLES AND ENJOY

2 Add the chicken stock, tamari, honey, sesame oil, and chili paste to the large saucepan, then bring to a boil on the stovetop over high heat. (Adjust the amount of chili paste to your liking to make the dish more or less spicy.)

3 Turn the heat down to medium and add the noodles. Simmer until the noodles are cooked and tender. (Check the packaging for the recommended cooking time, which will vary depending upon the brand.) Stir the noodles occasionally to prevent them from sticking together.

4 Sprinkle the green onion coins on top and serve hot.

CHEF TIP
If the ramen noodles come in small "bricks," use two forks to tease the noodles apart once they start to soften in the boiling broth.

47

SUSHI BOWL

MAKES: 4 servings **PREP TIME:** 30 minutes **COOK TIME:** 20 minutes

These colorful bowls combine elements of Japanese sushi and Hawaiian poke (pronounced POKE-ay). The seasoned rice is undeniably Japanese, while the deconstructed bowl of tasty toppings is a hallmark of poke. Each bite has an exciting combination of salty and slightly sweet flavors. If you're in a hurry, you can use precooked shrimp to make this meal quickly.

INGREDIENTS

RICE

1 cup (200 g) sushi rice (Japanese short-grain white rice)

1 cup (240 ml) water

2 tablespoons GF rice vinegar

1 tablespoon sugar

½ teaspoon salt

TOPPINGS

12 cooked shrimp, peeled, deveined, and tails removed (see Shrimp Cocktail, page 68, or use store-bought precooked shrimp)

1 cucumber

1 ripe avocado

1 tablespoon sesame seeds

2 tablespoons plus 2 teaspoons GF tamari soy sauce

SAUCE

2 tablespoons mayonnaise

1 teaspoon sriracha

¼ teaspoon sesame oil

TOOLS

Digital kitchen scale or measuring cups

Measuring spoons

Colander

Medium saucepan with a lid

Small saucepan

Large spoon

Large glass or wooden bowl (not metal)

Cutting board

Chef's knife (see Knives, page 8)

Vegetable peeler

Small bowl

MAKE THE RICE

1 Rinse the rice in the colander in the sink under cold water until the water runs clear.

2 Add the drained rice and the water to the medium saucepan and bring to a boil on the stovetop over high heat. Reduce the heat to medium-low, then cover with the lid. Simmer, covered, for 15 minutes, until all of the water has been absorbed.

3 While the rice is cooking, heat the vinegar, sugar, and salt in the small saucepan on the stovetop over medium heat, stirring with the large spoon until the sugar and salt dissolve. Turn off the heat, move the saucepan to a cool burner, and set it aside until the rice finishes cooking.

4 When the rice is done, use the spoon to scrape it into the large bowl. Immediately pour the vinegar mixture over it. Fold the rice with the spoon until it's evenly coated with the vinegar mixture. Leave the rice to cool to room temperature.

PREP THE TOPPINGS

5 On the cutting board, use the chef's knife to chop the shrimp into small, bite-size pieces.

6 Rinse the cucumber, then use the vegetable peeler to peel it. On the cutting board, use the chef's knife to dice the cucumber into small cubes. (If it's a large cucumber, after peeling it, cut it in half lengthwise, then use a spoon to scrape out the seeds from the center. This will leave a cucumber "boat." Dice the remaining cucumber.)

7 For instructions on how to cut the avocado and remove the pit, see Avocado Toast (page 28). Scoop out the avocado flesh from each half in one piece and dice it into small cubes.

8 In the small bowl, stir together the mayonnaise, sriracha, and sesame oil to make the sauce.

ASSEMBLE AND SERVE

9 Divide the rice among 4 serving bowls, ¾ cup (150 g) in each bowl. Divide the shrimp, cucumber, and avocado on top of the rice. Top each with a sprinkle of sesame seeds and about 2 teaspoons tamari. Finish each with a dollop of sauce.

MAKE IT YOUR OWN:

You can mix and match other toppings, if you like. Add sliced mango, sliced jalapeño chile, shredded carrot—the possibilities are endless!

CAPRESE CHICKEN SANDWICH

MAKES: 4 servings **PREP TIME:** 20 minutes

A caprese is an Italian combination of flavors that includes fresh basil, fresh tomato, and fresh mozzarella cheese (sort of like a margherita pizza)! As part of a chicken sandwich, it's *delizioso*.

INGREDIENTS

8 slices GF sandwich bread

8 ounces (227 g) fresh mozzarella (1 large ball)

1 large tomato

2 garlic cloves

½ lemon (about 1 tablespoon juice)

½ cup (112 g) mayonnaise

20 large basil leaves

¼ teaspoon salt

½ pound (227 g) deli-sliced chicken breast

TOOLS

Digital kitchen scale or measuring cups

Measuring spoons

Cutting board

Chef's knife (see Knives, page 8)

Citrus juicer, optional but recommended

Blender or food processor

Rubber spatula

DO THE PREP

1 Use a toaster or the oven to toast the slices of bread until they're as brown and crispy as you like.

2 On the cutting board, use the chef's knife to cut the mozzarella into 8 slices.

3 Rinse the tomato, then use the tip of the knife to cut the stem out of the top. Cut the tomato into 8 thin slices.

4 Peel the papery skin off the garlic cloves (see page 12).

MAKE THE BASIL SAUCE

5 Put the lemon half in the citrus juicer and squeeze out the juice into the blender or food processor. (If you don't have a citrus juicer, you can squeeze the lemon, cut side down, with your hand until the juice comes out.) Add the mayonnaise, basil, garlic, and salt to the lemon juice. Blend until smooth and light green in color.

6 Stop the blender and use the rubber spatula to scrape down the sides of the container. Blend again to make sure all the ingredients are well combined.

ASSEMBLE THE SANDWICHES

7 Lay out the slices of toast on the cutting board. Use the spatula to spread a layer of the sauce, about 1 tablespoon, on one side of each slice.

8 Divide the chicken evenly among 4 of the slices of toast.

9 Top the chicken with 2 slices of mozzarella each, then 2 slices of tomato.

10 Put the remaining slices of toast on top, sauce side down.

SERVE AND ENJOY

11 Slice the sandwiches in half. Serve and enjoy.

CHICKEN SALAD LETTUCE CUPS

MAKES: 4 servings   **PREP TIME:** 30 minutes

When you're looking for a light and fresh lunch that won't leave you hungry 20 minutes later, these lettuce cups will do the trick! The chicken salad has bright flavors that taste like summer. If you're using the Lemon-Herb Baked Chicken (page 79), make sure you plan ahead to have the cooked chicken on hand.

INGREDIENTS

½ recipe Lemon-Herb Baked Chicken (page 79) or 2 chicken breasts from a store-bought rotisserie chicken

8 seedless grapes

2 green onions

8 cilantro sprigs

4 parsley sprigs

¼ cup (28 g) slivered almonds

½ lemon (about 1 tablespoon juice)

¼ cup (75 g) plain Greek yogurt

2 tablespoons mayonnaise

1 tablespoon Dijon mustard

¼ teaspoon salt

⅛ teaspoon black pepper

8 butter lettuce leaves

TOOLS

Digital kitchen scale or measuring cups

Measuring spoons

Cutting board

Chef's knife (see Knives, page 8)

Large bowl

Large spoon

Citrus juicer, optional but recommended

Small bowl

Whisk

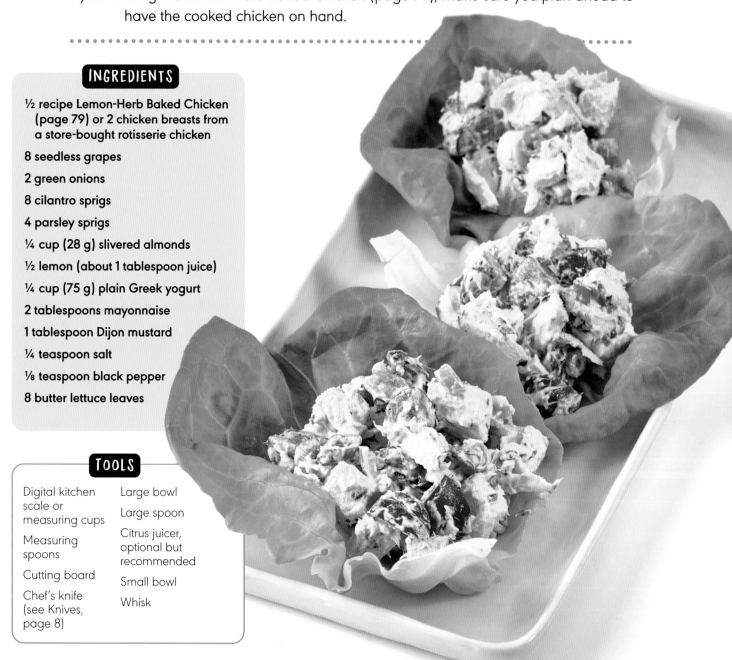

DO THE PREP

1 On the cutting board, use the chef's knife to dice the chicken into small pieces (see page 8). Put the chicken in the large bowl.

2 Rinse the grapes. Use the chef's knife to cut each one into quarters, then cut each quarter in half. Add to the chicken.

3 Rinse the green onions. Lay them on the cutting board and use the chef's knife to cut off the root ends and slice the green onions into thin coins. Add to the chicken.

4 Rinse the cilantro sprigs. Pull the leaves off the stems. (Put the stems in a compost bin if you have one.) On the cutting board, use the chef's knife to chop the leaves. Add the chopped cilantro to the chicken.

5 Rinse the parsley sprigs. Pull the leaves off the stems. (Put the stems in a compost bin if you have one.) On the cutting board, use the chef's knife to chop the leaves. Add the chopped parsley to the chicken.

6 Add the almonds to the chicken. Use the spoon to stir everything together.

7 Put the lemon half in the citrus juicer and squeeze out the juice into the small bowl. (If you don't have a citrus juicer, you can use your hand to squeeze the lemon, cut side down, until the juice comes out.)

8 Add the yogurt, mayonnaise, mustard, salt, and pepper to the lemon juice. Whisk to combine to make the dressing.

ASSEMBLE AND SERVE

9 Pour the dressing over the chicken salad and stir with the spoon to coat everything evenly.

10 Wash and dry the salad leaves. Spread the leaves out on a platter or plate.

11 Use the spoon to fill each leaf with the chicken salad. Serve right away, or refrigerate the chicken salad cups until you are ready to serve.

BLAT

MAKES: 4 servings **PREP TIME:** 20 minutes

Apart from simply being fun to say, BLAT is short for bacon, lettuce, avocado, and tomato. It's a sandwich packed with yummy flavor that will have you craving seconds.

INGREDIENTS

- 8 slices GF sandwich bread
- 1 large tomato
- 4 lettuce leaves (like green leaf, red leaf, romaine, Boston, or Bibb)
- 1 ripe avocado
- ¼ teaspoon salt
- 8 strips bacon, cooked (see Bacon and Sausage, page 32)

TOOLS

Measuring spoons

Cutting board

Chef's knife
(see Knives, page 8)

Salad spinner or 2 clean kitchen towels

Large spoon

Small bowl

Fork

Butter knife

DO THE PREP

1 Using a toaster or the oven, toast the bread until it's light golden brown. Set the toast aside.

2 Rinse the tomato. On the cutting board, use the tip of your chef's knife to cut the stem out of the top of the tomato. Slice the tomato into 8 thin slices. (For a helpful picture, see Caprese Chicken Sandwich, page 50.)

3 Rinse the lettuce leaves. You can use a salad spinner and spin them dry. Or lay the lettuce leaves on a clean kitchen towel, place another kitchen towel on top of the leaves, and loosely roll them up in the towel to dry them.

4 For instructions on how to cut the avocado and remove the pit, see Avocado Toast (page 28). Scoop the avocado flesh out of each half into the small bowl. Add the salt and mash with the fork to until the avocado is mostly smooth.

ASSEMBLE THE SANDWICHES

5 Lay out the toast. Using the butter knife, spread the mashed avocado on 4 of the slices.

6 Place 2 strips bacon on top of the avocado on each slice of toast. Break the bacon in half if the strips are too long to fit.

7 Top each with 2 tomato slices, then place a lettuce leaf on top of the tomato.

8 Top each sandwich with another slice of toast.

SERVE AND ENJOY

9 Slice the sandwiches in half, using the chef's knife. Serve up on plates and enjoy.

SNACKS

STRAWBERRY-BANANA SMOOTHIE

MAKES: 2 servings   **PREP TIME:** 5 minutes

This smoothie is a refreshing energy boost in a glass. Banana and your choice of milk make it satisfyingly creamy, Greek yogurt packs it with a punch of protein, and more fresh fruit and a touch of honey make it perfectly sweet.

Peel the banana and add it to the blender. Add the strawberries, yogurt, milk, and honey. Put the lid on and blend until smooth. Stop the blender and use the rubber spatula to scrape down the sides, if it is not completely mixed, and blend for a few more seconds. Pour into glasses and enjoy!

INGREDIENTS

1 ripe banana

2 cups (280 g) frozen strawberries

¼ cup (60 g) Greek yogurt

½ cup (120 ml) milk

1 tablespoon honey

TOOLS

Digital kitchen scale or measuring cups

Measuring spoons

Blender

Rubber spatula

MAKE IT YOUR OWN:

Switch up the flavors with other fruits and even vegetables while keeping the yogurt, milk, and honey the same! Some of our favorite combinations are:

Blueberry, banana, and spinach

Pineapple, mango, and carrot

Peach and strawberry

CRUMBLED GRANOLA

MAKES: 4 cups (8 servings)   **PREP TIME:** 10 minutes   **COOK TIME:** 30 minutes

Granola is a great on-the-go snack for adventures inside and outside your kitchen. Enjoy it plain, as part of a school lunch, or as your trail mix when out for a hike. Serve it in a bowl of milk instead of cereal for breakfast. Pair it with some yogurt and fresh fruit for a parfait. Or sprinkle some over a serving of applesauce to make a quick apple crumble.

DO THE PREP

1 Preheat the oven to 325°F (165°C).

2 Line the bottom of the baking pan with a piece of parchment paper. It's OK if the parchment paper goes up the sides of the pan.

MAKE THE GRANOLA

3 In the bowl, stir together the oats, almonds, pepitas, sunflower seeds, cinnamon, salt, ginger, and nutmeg.

4 Drizzle with the oil, agave nectar, and vanilla. Stir until everything is evenly coated.

BAKE THE GRANOLA

5 Pour the mixture into the prepared baking pan and spread it in an even layer with the spoon.

6 Put the baking pan in the oven. Bake for 15 minutes.

7 Wearing oven mitts, carefully remove the baking pan from the oven and stir the granola. Return the pan to the oven and bake for 15 minutes more, until the granola is golden brown.

SERVE AND ENJOY

8 Wearing oven mitts, carefully remove the baking pan from the oven, and let the granola cool to room temperature.

9 Break the cooled granola into small pieces. Serve and enjoy some right away. Store the rest in an airtight container for up to 1 week.

MAKE IT YOUR OWN:

Come up with your own granola flavor combinations by replacing the almonds, pepitas, and sunflower seeds with your choice of pecans, hazelnuts, pistachios, sesame seeds, or flaxseeds. Or you can add dried fruit like raisins, Craisins, mango, or apricot—or even chocolate chips! Just add the dried fruit or chocolate after the granola comes out of the oven.

INGREDIENTS

- 2 cups (216 g) GF old-fashioned rolled oats
- ½ cup (64 g) slivered almonds
- ¼ cup (38 g) unsalted pepitas (pumpkin seeds)
- ¼ cup (36 g) unsalted shelled sunflower seeds
- 1 teaspoon ground cinnamon
- ½ teaspoon salt
- ¼ teaspoon ground ginger
- ¼ teaspoon ground nutmeg
- ¼ cup (60 ml) olive oil
- ⅓ cup (111 g) agave nectar
- ½ teaspoon GF pure vanilla extract

TOOLS

Digital kitchen scale or measuring cups

Measuring spoons

9 x 13-inch (23 x 33 cm) baking pan

Parchment paper

Large bowl

Large spoon

Oven mitts

59

HUMMUS

MAKES: 2 cups (8 servings)   **PREP TIME:** 15 minutes

Hummus is a Middle Eastern dip or spread made of chickpeas (also known as garbanzo beans), tahini (sesame seed paste), lemon juice, and garlic. It pairs equally well with GF crackers and veggies, and you can make it in just a few minutes using a food processor.

DO THE PREP

1 Rinse the vegetables. Peel and slice the larger ones (like cucumbers) using the vegetable peeler, cutting board, and chef's knife. Put them on a plate along with the crackers.

2 Peel the papery skin off the garlic clove (see page 12).

3 Place a colander in the sink. Open the can of chickpeas with the can opener, pour them into the colander, and rinse with cold water.

MAKE THE HUMMUS

4 Add the drained chickpeas to the food processor.

5 On the cutting board, use the chef's knife to cut the lemon in half at its equator. One at a time, put the lemon halves in the citrus juicer and squeeze out the juice on top of the chickpeas. (If you don't have a citrus juicer, you can squeeze the lemon, cut side down, with your hand until the juice comes out.)

6 Add the oil, water, tahini, garlic, cumin, and salt to the chickpeas. Blend until smooth, 1 to 2 minutes.

SERVE AND ENJOY

7 Use the rubber spatula to scrape the hummus into a serving bowl. Be careful with the food processor blade because it is very sharp. Serve and enjoy with the prepared veggies and crackers.

INGREDIENTS

Veggies (like baby carrots, sugar snap peas, grape tomatoes, cucumber slices, or celery sticks)

GF crackers

1 small garlic clove

One 15-ounce can (425 g) no-salt-added chickpeas

1 small lemon (about 2 tablespoons juice)

¼ cup (60 ml) extra virgin olive oil

3 tablespoons cold water

3 tablespoons tahini, stirred well

½ teaspoon ground cumin

½ teaspoon salt

TOOLS

Can opener

Liquid measuring cup

Measuring spoons

Vegetable peeler

Cutting board

Chef's knife (see Knives, page 8)

Colander

Food processor

Citrus juicer, optional but recommended

Rubber spatula

POPCORN

MAKES: 6 cups (4 servings) **PREP TIME:** 1 minute
COOK TIME: 10 minutes

Could you buy bags of prepopped popcorn or microwave popcorn? Sure. But there's nothing quite like the taste of freshly popped popcorn made on the stovetop. Enjoy it plain or add some melted butter for a richer movie theater taste.

INGREDIENTS

2 tablespoons olive oil

¼ cup (54 g) popcorn kernels

2 tablespoons unsalted butter, melted (see page 12), optional

½ teaspoon salt

TOOLS

Measuring spoons

Digital kitchen scale or measuring cups

Medium saucepan with lid

Oven mitts

Large bowl

Large spoon

MAKE THE POPCORN

1 Add the oil to the saucepan and place it on the stovetop over medium-high heat. Drop 2 popcorn kernels into the oil and wait until 1 of the kernels pops. (This will tell you the oil is hot enough and ready to pop all the popcorn.)

2 Add the rest of the popcorn kernels to the oil, cover the saucepan with its lid, and leave it to cook over medium-high heat. After a few minutes, you'll start to hear the kernels vigorously popping.

3 Once the popping slows down to about one pop per second, give the saucepan a gentle shake to move any uncooked kernels to the bottom. As soon as there is no more popping for 3 seconds, turn off the heat and move the saucepan to a cool burner. Remove the lid and pour the popcorn into the bowl.

SERVE AND ENJOY

4 If you would like to add butter, melt it in the microwave or on the stovetop (see page 12). Drizzle it over the popcorn.

5 Sprinkle the popcorn with the salt and stir to distribute the salt over all the popcorn. Serve and enjoy.

5-MINUTE TOMATO SALSA

MAKES: 1½ cups (6 servings)   **PREP TIME:** 10 minutes

Tomato salsa—often paired with corn tortilla chips—is a classic, naturally gluten-free snack. And while store-bought jarred salsas are convenient, it's hard to compete with the bright flavors of a fresh salsa. This recipe gives you the best of both worlds: It's quick to make with canned tomatoes and a food processor or blender, but fresh ingredients—onion, jalapeño chile, cilantro, and lime juice—will take your taste buds straight to Mexico. Serve with your favorite GF tortilla chips.

INGREDIENTS

One 14.5-ounce (411 g) can diced tomatoes

1 medium onion

1 jalapeño chile

1 garlic clove

¼ cup (10 g) packed cilantro leaves and stems

½ lime (about 1 tablespoon juice)

¼ teaspoon ground cumin

¼ teaspoon salt

TOOLS

Can opener

Digital kitchen scale or measuring cups

Measuring spoons

Food processor

Cutting board

Chef's knife (see Knives, page 8)

Citrus juicer, optional but recommended

DO THE PREP

1 Use the can opener to open the tomatoes, then add the tomatoes and the liquid from the can to the food processor.

2 Place the onion on the cutting board and use the chef's knife to cut it in half from top to bottom (through the shoot and root ends). Lay the halves flat and cut them in half again, shoot to root, to make four quarters. Take one of the onion quarters and cut off the top and bottom, and remove the papery outer skin. Add the cleaned onion quarter to the tomatoes. Save the remaining three quarters of the onion for another dish (see page 11).

3 Rinse the jalapeño, then cut it in half lengthwise. Scrape out all the seeds from one half. If you like spicy salsa, add the full half of the jalapeño. If you prefer milder salsa, cut the half in half and use just a quarter (see Tip).

CHEF TIP

Be careful not to touch your face, especially your eyes and nose, when working with a spicy chile. The oils can burn! Wash your hands well with soap after handling.

FINISH AND SERVE

4 Peel the papery skin off the garlic clove (see page 12). Add the garlic to the tomatoes.

5 Put the lime half in the citrus juicer and squeeze out the juice on top of the tomatoes. (If you don't have a citrus juicer, you can use your hand to squeeze the lime, cut side down, until juice comes out.)

6 Add the cilantro, cumin, and salt to the tomatoes. Blend until smooth. Being careful with the food processor blade, transfer to a serving bowl and enjoy.

TOMATILLO-CHIPOTLE SALSA

MAKES: 1½ cups (6 servings)   **PREP TIME:** 5 minutes   **COOK TIME:** 8 to 9 minutes

Supermarket salsas usually come in three options: mild, medium, and hot. Most of them start with a base of just tomatoes. This recipe gives you an exciting alternative, using green tomatillos and a smoky chipotle chile (a fire-roasted jalapeño chile). Serve with your favorite GF tortilla chips.

DO THE PREP

1 Remove the papery husks from the tomatillos. Rinse the tomatillos to remove stickiness. Rinse the tomato.

2 Move an oven rack to the top position and turn on the broiler.

COOK THE INGREDIENTS

3 Place the tomatillos, tomato, and garlic cloves in the baking pan. Put the pan under the broiler for 4 minutes, until the tops of the vegetables are soft, with a few black spots.

4 Wearing oven mitts, carefully remove the baking pan from the oven. Use the tongs to remove the garlic cloves and set them aside to cool, and to turn the tomatillos and tomato over.

5 Return the baking pan to the oven and broil the tomatillos and tomato for another 4 to 5 minutes, until the second side is soft, with black spots. (The skins will split and some liquid will come out of the tomatillos and tomato—that's OK.)

FINISH THE SALSA AND ENJOY

6 Wearing oven mitts, carefully take the baking pan out of the oven and use the tongs to add them to the blender along with any liquid in the baking pan.

7 Peel the papery skin off the garlic cloves (see page 12) and add to the roasted tomatillos and tomato.

8 Add the chipotle and salt to the blender. Blend until smooth. Serve warm or allow to cool to room temperature.

INGREDIENTS

6 tomatillos

1 tomato

4 garlic cloves

1 GF chipotle chile in adobo sauce (from a small can)

½ teaspoon salt

TOOLS

Can opener

Measuring spoons

9-inch (23 cm) square baking pan

Oven mitts

Tongs

Blender

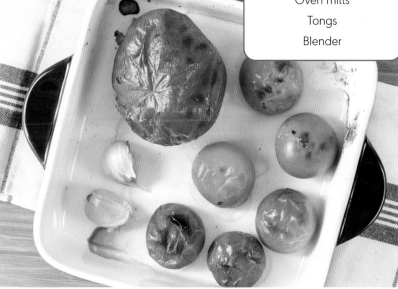

GUACAMOLE

MAKES: 1½ cups (6 servings) **PREP TIME:** 5 minutes

A homemade creamy guacamole is the perfect addition to all kinds of dishes. Have it as a snack with some gluten-free tortilla chips. Put a dollop on your tacos. Spread it on a slice of gluten-free toast. When your avocados are ripe, make this recipe!

INGREDIENTS

2 ripe avocados

½ lime (about 1 tablespoon juice)

½ teaspoon salt

¼ teaspoon garlic powder

¼ teaspoon onion powder

1 tablespoon chopped cilantro, optional

TOOLS

Measuring spoons

Chef's knife
(see Knives, page 8)

Large spoon

Medium bowl

Citrus juicer, optional but recommended

Fork or potato masher

DO THE PREP

1 For instructions on how to cut the avocados and remove the pits, see Avocado Toast (page 28). Using the large spoon, scoop the flesh from the avocados into the bowl.

MAKE THE GUACAMOLE AND SERVE

2 Put the lime half in the citrus juicer and squeeze out the juice on top of the avocados. (If you don't have a citrus juicer, you can use your hand to squeeze the lime, cut side down, until juice comes out.)

3 Add the salt, garlic powder, and onion powder to the avocado. Use the fork or potato masher to mash and mix everything together until the guacamole is mostly smooth.

4 Add the cilantro, if you like, and stir to combine. Serve right away.

BRUSCHETTA

MAKES: 20 pieces **PREP TIME:** 20 minutes **COOK TIME:** 8 to 10 minutes

This classic Italian dish works great as either a standalone snack or as an appetizer before a larger meal. It tops crostini (thin slices of lightly toasted white bread) with bruschetta (a fresh mixture of Mediterranean ingredients including tomato, basil, garlic, and extra virgin olive oil).

● ●

MAKE THE CROSTINI

1 Preheat the oven to 400°F (200°C).

2 On the cutting board, use the serrated knife to slice the baguette into about twenty ½-inch (13 mm) slices. Lay the slices on a rimmed baking sheet in a single layer.

3 Drizzle the oil over the bread. Then sprinkle with the garlic powder, salt, and pepper.

4 Bake for 8 to 10 minutes, until the bread starts to brown on the edges.

5 Wearing oven mitts, carefully remove the baking sheet from the oven and set it aside to cool.

DO THE PREP AND MAKE THE BRUSCHETTA TOPPING

6 Rinse the tomatoes and basil leaves.

7 On the cutting board, use the chef's knife to cut the tomatoes in half, then cut each half into quarters to make 8 pieces. Place in the small bowl.

8 Use the chef's knife and cutting board to chop the basil into small pieces. Add the basil to the tomatoes.

9 Peel the papery skin off the garlic clove (see page 12).

10 Squeeze the garlic through the garlic press into the bowl with the tomatoes and basil. (If you don't have a garlic press, mince the garlic on the cutting board with the chef's knife and scrape the garlic into the tomatoes and basil.)

11 Add the oil, vinegar, salt, and pepper to the tomatoes and stir with the large spoon to combine.

ASSEMBLE AND SERVE

12 Heap the crostini on a platter and serve next to the bowl of bruschetta topping. Use a spoon to top the crostini with the bruschetta topping as you eat. This prevents the crostini from getting soggy.

INGREDIENTS

CROSTINI

One GF baguette (about 10 inches/25 cm long)

2 tablespoons olive oil

1 teaspoon garlic powder

½ teaspoon salt

¼ teaspoon black pepper

BRUSCHETTA TOPPING

1 pint (304 g) grape tomatoes

8 basil leaves

1 small garlic clove

1 tablespoon extra virgin olive oil

1 teaspoon balsamic vinegar

⅛ teaspoon salt

⅛ teaspoon black pepper

TOOLS

Measuring spoons

Cutting board

Serrated knife

Rimmed baking sheet

Oven mitts

Chef's knife (see Knives, page 8)

Small bowl

Garlic press, optional

Large spoon

65

QUICKLES

MAKES: 2 cups (about 8 servings)
PREP TIME: 10 minutes   **CHILL TIME:** at least 30 minutes

As you might guess from the name, this recipe is a way to make your own "quick pickles." *Quickles*, get it? They're great on their own as a snack and as a side to accompany a larger meal—try them with Hamburger Sliders (page 96)!

INGREDIENTS

½ cup (120 ml) GF rice vinegar

¼ cup (50 g) sugar

2 tablespoons GF tamari soy sauce

1 teaspoon sesame oil

½ teaspoon ground ginger

2 small (6-8 inches/15-20 cm) zucchini or 1 seedless English cucumber

TOOLS

Digital kitchen scale or measuring cups

Measuring spoons

Small saucepan

Spoon

2-cup (480 ml) container or jar with a lid

Cutting board

Chef's knife
(see Knives, page 8)

DO THE PREP

1 In the saucepan, add the rice vinegar, sugar, tamari, sesame oil, and ginger. Stir to combine. Heat on the stovetop over low heat until the sugar has dissolved, about 5 minutes.

2 Pour the mixture into the container.

3 Wash the zucchini.

FINISH AND ENJOY

4 On the cutting board, use the chef's knife to cut the ends off the zucchini, then slice into round coins about ⅛-inch (3 mm) thick.

5 Add the coins to the vinegar mixture and cover the container with its lid. Refrigerate for 30 minutes before serving.

6 Enjoy fresh, or refrigerate and keep for up to 1 week.

FANCY CRACKERS

MAKES: 2 servings **PREP TIME:** 5 minutes

These days you can find lots of really good gluten-free crackers at many supermarkets. This recipe jazzes them up with rich, soft cheese and fig spread. You can also make this snack heartier with the addition of Genoa or other hard salami or thinly sliced prosciutto.

INGREDIENTS

6 GF crackers

2 ounces (57 g) soft cheese (like Brie, Fromager d'Affinois, or Brillat-Savarin)*

1 tablespoon fig spread

TOOLS

Measuring spoons

Butter knife

Spoon

Set the crackers on a plate. Spread the cheese on the crackers with the butter knife. Use the spoon to top each with a ½-teaspoon dollop of fig spread.

*These cheeses can be found in the specialty cheese section near the deli at the super-market, not in the refrigerator packaged cheese section with the rest of the dairy.

67

SHRIMP COCKTAIL

MAKES: 4 servings   **PREP TIME:** 15 minutes   **COOK TIME:** 3 to 5 minutes

Shrimp cocktail is a dish that often looks and sounds fancy, but it's surprisingly easy to make. Impress your family and friends with this tasty snack, complete with a semi-homemade cocktail sauce. They never have to know your secret!

INGREDIENTS

SHRIMP

3 quarts (3 L) water

1 tablespoon salt

Ice

1 pound (20 to 25 shrimp/450 g) raw deveined shell-on jumbo shrimp, fresh or frozen

COCKTAIL SAUCE AND LEMON WEDGES

½ cup (136 g) ketchup

½ lemon (about 1 tablespoon juice)

1 to 2 teaspoons prepared horseradish

1 whole lemon

TOOLS

Measuring spoons

Digital kitchen scale or measuring cups

Large saucepan

Large bowl

Colander

Whisk

Small bowl

Cutting board

Chef's knife (see Knives, page 8)

Paper towels

DO THE PREP

1 Add the water and salt to the saucepan, then bring it to a boil on the stovetop over high heat.

2 Fill the large bowl with ice and add enough cold water to cover the ice.

3 Place the colander in the sink.

COOK THE SHRIMP

4 When the water is at a rolling boil, add the shrimp, and boil for 3 to 5 minutes. The shrimp will begin to float and will turn pink. To test for doneness, cut 1 shrimp in half. The interior should be completely opaque (white), no longer translucent (a clear-ish light gray).

5 Carefully pour the water and cooked shrimp into the colander to drain. Immediately pour the drained shrimp from the colander into the bowl of ice water to cool completely while you make the sauce.

MAKE THE SAUCE AND LEMON WEDGES

6 Whisk together the ketchup, lemon juice, and horseradish in the small bowl.

7 Wash the lemon. On the cutting board, use the chef's knife to cut the lemon into wedges: Cut the lemon in half from top to bottom, not around the equator. Cut each half into four wedges.

FINISH AND SERVE

8 If the shrimp are already peeled, skip to the next step. Peel the shells off the cooled shrimp. You can leave the tails on if you want, but it's also OK to take the tails off and serve the shrimp completely peeled.

9 Place the peeled shrimp on a paper towel and pat them dry with a second paper towel. Arrange the shrimp on a plate along with the cocktail sauce and lemon wedges. Serve cold. (Cover and refrigerate the plate if you're not serving the shrimp right away.)

DINNER

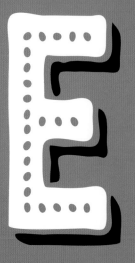

RED LENTIL DAL

MAKES: 4 servings **PREP TIME:** 15 minutes **COOK TIME:** 25 minutes

Dal, a lentil dish of Indian origin, is packed with flavorful spices without being spicy. You can easily make it vegetarian (or vegan) by substituting vegetable stock for the chicken stock. Serve over Oven-Baked Rice (page 105).

INGREDIENTS

1 cup (200 g) red lentils

1 small onion

2 teaspoons curry powder

½ teaspoon ground ginger

¼ teaspoon ground cumin

¼ teaspoon garlic powder

8 cilantro sprigs

1 tablespoon olive oil

2 cups (480 ml) GF chicken stock or broth

¼ teaspoon salt

TOOLS

Digital kitchen scale or measuring cups

Measuring spoons

Colander

Cutting board

Chef's knife
(see Knives, page 8)

Small bowl

Salad spinner or kitchen towel

Medium saucepan with lid

Large spoon

Immersion blender or food processor

DO THE PREP

1 Pour the lentils into a colander in the sink and rinse them under cold water. Leave the lentils in the colander to drain.

2 Dice the onion using the chef's knife and cutting board:

1 First cut the top (shoot end) off the onion.

2 Place the cut side on the cutting board and cut the onion in half, starting at the root end, down to the cutting board.

3 Peel the papery skin off each half.

4 Place one half on the cutting board, cut side down, and carefully make parallel vertical cuts about ½ inch (13 mm) apart, without going through the root.

5 Rotate the onion and make parallel vertical slices in the other direction also about ½ inch (13 mm) apart, this time cutting the root end off.

6 Repeat with the second onion half, then place all of the diced onion in the medium bowl.

3 Stir together the curry powder, ginger, cumin, and garlic in the small bowl.

4 Rinse the cilantro. Take the leaves off the stems and chop them on the cutting board. (Compost the stems, if you can.) Leave the chopped cilantro on the cutting board to use later.

COOK THE DAL

5 Add the oil to the saucepan and heat it on the stovetop over medium-high heat for about 30 seconds. Add the onions and cook until they're soft and translucent, about 5 minutes. Stir occasionally so all the onions cook evenly.

6 Add the mixed spices and cook, stirring frequently, until the spices are very fragrant, 2 minutes more.

7 Add the drained lentils and the chicken stock. Bring to a simmer, turn the heat down to medium-low, and cover with the lid. Cook for 15 minutes.

8 Remove the lid. Stir the lentils and check to see if they're very soft. If they're not falling apart when you stir them, re-cover the saucepan and cook them for 5 minutes more. Turn off the heat and move the saucepan to a cool burner.

FINISH THE DAL

9 Use an immersion blender in the saucepan to blend the lentils until smooth. (If you do not have an immersion blender, transfer the lentils to a food processor and blend until smooth or enjoy them without pureeing.)

10 Add the cilantro and salt and stir to combine. Serve hot.

PIZZA

MAKES: 8 slices **PREP AND RISE TIME:** 25 minutes **COOK TIME:** 12 to 15 minutes

Did you know that Americans eat an average of 23 pounds (more than 10 kg) of pizza *per person* each year? We can't blame them. After all, pizza is one of the most popular foods in the world! And with this recipe, you can enjoy a few slices—or a whole pie—too. Spice up your pizza with your favorite toppings, like sliced pepperoni or mushrooms.

INGREDIENTS

- ¾ cup (180 ml) warm water, about 115°F (45°C)
- 2 teaspoons sugar
- 1 teaspoon active dry yeast
- 1½ cups (187 g) GF all-purpose flour blend
- 1 teaspoon salt
- ¼ teaspoon xanthan gum
- 1 tablespoon olive oil, plus more for pressing out the dough
- ¼ cup (60 g) tomato sauce
- 2 big handfuls (6 ounces/170 g) shredded mozzarella
- ¼ teaspoon dried basil
- ¼ teaspoon dried oregano

TOOLS

Digital kitchen scale or measuring cups	Parchment paper
Measuring spoons	Baking sheet
Small bowl	Spoon
Whisk	Cutting board
Medium bowl	Pizza cutter or chef's knife
Rubber spatula	

MAKE THE DOUGH

1 In the small bowl, whisk together the warm water, sugar, and yeast. Set aside until the mixture is foamy and the yeast is active, about 5 minutes.

2 Meanwhile, in the medium bowl, whisk together the flour, salt, and xanthan gum.

3 Whisk the oil into the yeast mixture. Then add the yeast mixture to the flour mixture. Stir vigorously with the spoon to form a smooth, wet dough.

SHAPE THE DOUGH

4 Place a 15-inch (38 cm) square piece of parchment paper on the counter. Scrape the dough onto the middle of the paper, using the rubber spatula.

5 Coat your hands generously with oil and press the dough out into a 12-inch (30 cm) circle. Leave the dough slightly thicker around the edge. Slide the baking sheet *under* the parchment paper with pressed-out dough.

CHEF TIP
You know your yeast is alive if you see bubbles.

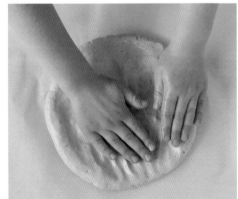

DINNER

6 Leave the dough to rise on the counter for 15 minutes. While it's rising, move an oven rack to the lowest position and preheat the oven to 500°F (260°C).

TOP THE PIZZA AND BAKE

7 After the dough has risen, spoon the tomato sauce onto the dough and carefully spread it out evenly. Leave the edge of the dough bare.

8 Sprinkle on the cheese, basil, and oregano. Add any other toppings you like on top of the cheese and herbs.

9 Put the baking sheet in the oven. Bake for 12 to 15 minutes, until the cheese is melted and golden brown in places and the crust edge is golden.

SERVE AND ENJOY

10 Wearing oven mitts, carefully remove the baking sheet from the oven and allow the pizza to cool for a few minutes.

11 Slide the pizza off the parchment paper onto the cutting board. Compost or throw away the parchment paper. Using the pizza cutter or chef's knife, cut the pizza into 8 slices and serve warm!

CRISPY DOVER SOLE

MAKES: 4 servings   **PREP TIME:** 10 minutes   **COOK TIME:** 10 minutes

Dover sole is a flatfish native to the North Atlantic Ocean, with white, tender meat.
Coated in seasoned gluten-free flour and fried in a blend of olive oil and butter, these crispy fillets will
even have people who don't like fish saying, "More, please!" (Many seafood markets also offer Pacific
sole, which is similar but actually a flounder. It's a great and affordable option, too.)
Serve with Roasted Veggies (page 108) and Oven-Baked Rice (page 105).

INGREDIENTS

⅓ cup (42 g) GF all-purpose flour blend

¾ teaspoon salt

¼ teaspoon black pepper

8 Dover sole fillets (about ¾ pound/340 g)

2 tablespoons olive oil

2 tablespoons unsalted butter

TOOLS

Digital kitchen scale or measuring cups

Measuring spoons

2 large plates

Paper towels

Large skillet

Spatula

Wire rack

DO THE PREP

1 Add the flour, salt, and pepper to one of the plates and mix to combine.

2 Rinse the fish fillets and pat them dry with paper towels.

3 Coat both sides of each fillet in the flour mixture, shaking off any excess flour, and place on the second plate. Wash your hands!

COOK THE SOLE

4 Heat the skillet on the stovetop over medium-high heat for 1 to 2 minutes, until a drop of water sizzles when you drop it in the skillet (see page 117).

5 Add 1 tablespoon each of the oil and butter to the hot skillet. Allow the butter to melt completely and start to sizzle.

6 Add 4 of the fish fillets to the skillet. Cook on the first side about 2 minutes, until golden brown on the bottom. Use the spatula to lift the edge of one fillet and peek at the bottom. If it's golden brown, it's ready to flip.

7 Use the spatula to carefully flip the fillets. Cook on the second side until golden brown, about 2 minutes more.

8 Remove the fillets from the skillet with the spatula and place them on the wire rack to rest while you cook the remaining fillets (see Tip).

9 Add the remaining 1 tablespoon oil and 1 tablespoon butter to the skillet. Repeat steps 6 through 8 until all of the fish is cooked.

10 Serve right away, while the fish is warm and crispy.

CHEF TIP
Cooling the sole on a wire rack keeps the bottom of the fillets from getting soggy.

LEMON-HERB BAKED CHICKEN

MAKES: 4 servings   **PREP TIME:** 5 minutes   **COOK TIME:** 25 to 30 minutes

This chicken is a great low-maintenance dinner option, since the oven does most of the work for you. By starting with boneless, skinless chicken breasts, you don't have to worry about carving a whole chicken when it comes out of the oven—it's already ready to slice and serve. Enjoy it hot with Roasted Veggies (page 108) and Roasted Potatoes (page 106), or cold, sliced on a salad from the Crunchy Crouton Salad Bar (page 112).

INGREDIENTS

- ½ lemon (about 1 tablespoon juice)
- 4 boneless, skinless chicken breasts (about 2 pounds/900 g)
- 1 tablespoon olive oil
- 1 teaspoon dried herbs (like basil, oregano, thyme, or a combination)
- ½ teaspoon salt
- ¼ teaspoon black pepper

TOOLS

Measuring spoons

Citrus juicer, optional but recommended

Medium bowl

Tongs

9 x 13-inch (23 x 33 cm) baking pan

Oven mitts

Instant-read meat thermometer

DO THE PREP

1. Preheat the oven to 400°F (200°C).

2. Put the lemon half in the citrus juicer and squeeze out the juice into the bowl (see Tip).

3. Place the chicken in the bowl with the lemon juice. Add the oil, herbs, salt, and pepper. Toss with your hands or tongs to evenly coat the chicken.

4. Place the chicken breasts in the baking pan so they're not touching each other. Wash your hands!

BAKE THE CHICKEN

5. Bake for 25 to 30 minutes, until the chicken is white all the way through when you cut into it, and the internal temperature reaches 165°F (75°C). (To test the temperature, wearing oven mitts, carefully remove the baking pan from the oven. Stick the instant-read meat thermometer into the thickest part of a chicken breast. If it goes up to 165°F/75°C, the chicken is done. If not, take the thermometer out and put the chicken back in the oven for a few minutes more. Then take its temperature again.)

DINNER

CHEF TIP
If you don't have a juicer, cup your hand under the lemon to catch the seeds.

CHICKEN NOODLE SOUP

MAKES: 4 servings   **PREP TIME:** 15 minutes   **COOK TIME:** 50 minutes

Whether you're home sick from school (no fun!) or it's a cold winter night, when it comes to "comfort food" is there anything better than old-fashioned chicken noodle soup? This soup will have you feeling warm and cozy in no time.

INGREDIENTS

1 medium onion

10 baby carrots

2 celery stalks

1 tablespoon olive oil

3 bone-in, skin-on chicken thighs (about 1 pound/450 g)

4 cups (1 L) GF chicken stock or broth

¾ teaspoon salt

1 cup (100 g) GF short macaroni pasta (like elbows, farfalle, or shells)

TOOLS

Measuring spoons

Digital kitchen scale or measuring cups

Chef's knife (see Knives, page 8)

Cutting board

Medium bowl

Spatula

Large saucepan with lid

Instant-read meat thermometer

Tongs

Plate

DO THE PREP

1 Dice the onion using the chef's knife and cutting board. (For instructions on how to dice the onion and a helpful picture, see Red Lentil Dal, page 72.) Place the diced onions in the bowl.

2 Cut each baby carrot in half lengthwise, then slice each half into half-moons. Add to the onions.

3 Cut the top and bottom off the celery stalks. Cut each stalk in half lengthwise, then slice into small pieces. Add to the onions and carrots.

COOK THE SOUP

4 Add the oil to the saucepan and heat on the stovetop over medium heat for about 30 seconds.

5 Add the onions, carrots, and celery and cook, stirring occasionally with the spatula, until they begin to soften, about 5 minutes.

6 Add the chicken thighs, chicken stock, and salt. Turn the heat up to high and bring to a boil, then turn the heat back down to medium. Cover with the lid and simmer until the chicken is cooked through and the internal temperature reaches 165°F (75°C), about 30 minutes (see Lemon-Herb Baked Chicken, page 79, for instructions on testing temperature).

80

FINISH THE SOUP

7 Remove the chicken thighs with the tongs and set them on the plate to cool.

8 Add the noodles to the soup, re-cover the saucepan, and cook until the noodles are tender, about 15 minutes. Stir the noodles every few minutes to prevent them from sticking together.

9 When the chicken is cool enough to handle, use your fingers to remove the skin and bones and shred the chicken meat. (Leave the skin, bones, and any pieces of fat behind to discard.) Add the shredded chicken back to the soup. Serve the soup hot.

PEANUT NOODLES WITH CHICKEN AND VEGGIES

MAKES: 4 to 6 servings   **PREP TIME:** 10 minutes   **COOK TIME:** 20 minutes

If you like the taste of peanut butter, you're going to *love* this dish. The pleasantly salty, peanut buttery noodles pair perfectly with the tasty chicken and veggies.

INGREDIENTS

10 baby carrots

20 sugar snap peas

2 boneless, skinless chicken breasts (about 1 pound/450 g)

¼ teaspoon salt

2 quarts (2 L) plus ½ cup (120 ml) water

¼ cup (66 g) smooth peanut butter

2 tablespoons GF rice vinegar

1 tablespoon packed brown sugar

¼ teaspoon garlic powder

¼ teaspoon ground ginger

1 tablespoon olive oil

3 tablespoons GF tamari soy sauce

8 ounces (227 g) pad thai rice noodles (¼-inch/6 mm wide)

TOOLS

Digital kitchen scale or measuring cups

Measuring spoons

Chef's knife (see Knives, page 8)

Cutting board

Small bowl

2 medium bowls

Whisk

Large saucepan

Large skillet

Spatula or tongs

Colander

Large spoon

DO THE PREP

1 Using the chef's knife and cutting board, cut each baby carrot in half lengthwise. Then cut each half into long, thin strips. Add the carrot strips to the small bowl.

2 If your sugar snap peas are not trimmed, you can trim them by snapping off the stem end and pulling the string away from the pea. Add the sugar snap peas to the carrot strips.

3 On the cutting board, use the chef's knife to cut each chicken breast into ½- to 1-inch-wide (13 mm to 2.5 cm) strips, then rotate the strips and slice them into ½- to 1-inch (13 mm to 2.5 cm) cubes. Place the chicken in one of the medium bowls. Wash your hands!

4 Sprinkle the salt on the chicken and stir.

MAKE THE SAUCE

5 In the other medium bowl, whisk together ½ cup (120 ml) water, the peanut butter, rice vinegar, brown sugar, garlic powder, and ground ginger to combine. (The peanut butter won't completely dissolve; that's OK.) Set the bowl aside.

COOK THE NOODLES, CHICKEN, AND VEGETABLES

6 Add the water and some salt to the saucepan, then bring it to a boil on the stovetop over high heat.

7 While the water is coming to a boil, heat the skillet on the stovetop over medium-high heat for 1 to 2 minutes, until a drop of water sizzles when you drop it in the skillet (see page 117).

8 Add the oil, then use the spatula or tongs to place the chicken in the skillet in a single layer. Leave the chicken to cook until it begins to brown on the bottom, about 2 minutes. Stir, then let it cook for 2 minutes more. Stir one more time. (This makes sure the chicken cooks evenly.)

9 When most of the moisture has evaporated from the chicken, add the sugar snap peas and carrots. Cook until the vegetables are tender and the chicken is completely white when you cut a cube in half (which means it is cooked through), about 3 minutes more.

10 Add the sauce, stir, and cook until heated through and slightly thickened, 3 to 4 minutes. Turn off the heat and move the skillet to a cool burner.

11 Add the noodles to the boiling water and cook until al dente (see Baked Mac and Cheese, page 43), 2 to 3 minutes. Stir the noodles every few minutes to prevent them from sticking together. While the noodles are cooking, place a colander in the sink.

12 Carefully pour the water and cooked noodles into the colander to drain.

FINISH AND SERVE

13 Add the drained noodles to the chicken and sauce. Stir everything together until the noodles are coated in the sauce. Serve hot.

CHICKEN AND VEGGIE LO MEIN

MAKES: 4 to 6 servings **PREP TIME:** 15 minutes **COOK TIME:** 20 minutes

Lo mein is a noodle dish that's a staple of Chinese takeout restaurants across America. It can be hard to find gluten-free versions, because it's usually made with wheat noodles. Thankfully, this recipe brings those same great flavors into your own kitchen using gluten-free spaghetti.

INGREDIENTS

3 quarts (3 L) plus 2 tablespoons water

1 teaspoon salt

1 broccoli crown

1 red bell pepper

2 boneless, skinless chicken breasts (about 1 pound/ 450 g)

12 ounces (340 g) GF spaghetti

2 tablespoons olive oil

MARINADE

1 tablespoon GF tamari soy sauce

1 teaspoon sesame oil

1 teaspoon GF Worcestershire sauce

SAUCE

¼ cup (60 ml) GF tamari soy sauce

2 tablespoons mirin

1 tablespoon cornstarch

2 teaspoons sesame oil

2 teaspoons GF Worcestershire sauce

TOOLS

Measuring spoons

Digital kitchen scale or measuring cups

Large saucepan

Chef's knife (see Knives, page 8)

Cutting board

3 medium bowls

2 large spoons

Small bowl

Whisk

Colander

Large skillet with lid

Tongs

Spatula

BOIL THE WATER FOR THE SPAGHETTI

1 Place a large saucepan with the water on the stovetop. Add the salt and heat over high heat until the water comes to a boil. (If the water comes to a boil before you've finished preparing the rest of the ingredients, turn the heat down to low and put the lid on the saucepan to keep the water hot.)

DO THE PREP

2 Rinse the broccoli. Use a chef's knife and cutting board to cut the broccoli crown apart into florets. If a floret is large, cut it in half until all the pieces are bite-size. Set it aside in one of the medium bowls.

3 Rinse the red bell pepper. Place it on its side on the cutting board, then cut a small amount off the top and bottom. Stand it up on the cut bottom, then cut the pepper in half. Remove all the seeds and membranes. Lay the two halves of the pepper on the cutting board, skin side down. Slice the two halves and bottom of the pepper into thin strips. Set aside in a second medium bowl.

4 Cut each chicken breast into thin strips. Put the chicken strips in the third medium bowl. Wash your hands!

MARINATE THE CHICKEN

5 Add the tamari, sesame oil, and Worcestershire sauce to the chicken. Stir with the spoon until the chicken is completely coated with the marinade. Keep the spoon in the bowl for later use.

MAKE THE SAUCE

6 In the small bowl, whisk together the tamari, mirin, cornstarch, sesame oil, and Worcestershire sauce until the cornstarch is dissolved in the liquid.

COOK THE SPAGHETTI

7 When the water comes to a boil, add the spaghetti and cook it until al dente (see Baked Mac and Cheese, page 42). Stir the spaghetti occasionally to prevent it from sticking together. While the spaghetti is cooking, place a colander in the sink.

8 When the spaghetti is cooked, carefully pour the water and spaghetti into the colander to drain. The spaghetti can rest in the colander until step 13.

COOK THE VEGETABLES AND CHICKEN

9 While the spaghetti is cooking, heat the skillet on the stovetop over medium-high heat for 1 to 2 minutes, until a drop of water sizzles when you drop it on the skillet (see page 117). Add the broccoli and 2 tablespoons water, cover with the lid, and cook until the broccoli is bright green, about 1 minute. Remove the lid. Cook until the water has evaporated, occasionally tossing the broccoli with the tongs.

10 Add 1 tablespoon of the oil and the sliced red pepper to the broccoli. Cook, tossing the vegetables occasionally with tongs, until they are tender, about 4 minutes. Transfer the veggies from the skillet to one of the empty medium bowls and set aside.

11 Add the remaining 1 tablespoon oil to the skillet, still over medium-high heat. Add the marinated chicken. Use the spatula to spread the chicken in a single layer. Leave the chicken to cook until it gets brown on the bottom, about 2 minutes. Using the same spatula, toss the chicken. Leave it to cook until it is cooked through and most of the liquid has evaporated, 2 to 3 minutes more. (Don't use the raw chicken spatula anymore; switch to the tongs you used for the vegetables.)

12 Add the cooked veggies to the chicken. Whisk the sauce again if the cornstarch has settled to the bottom of the bowl, then pour it over the chicken and veggies. Cook everything until the sauce thickens, about 1 minute. Turn off the heat.

13 Add the cooked spaghetti and toss everything together with the tongs to coat with the sauce. Serve hot.

ORANGE CHICKEN

MAKES: 4 to 6 servings   PREP TIME: 15 minutes   COOK TIME: 20 minutes

Like lo mein (see page 84), orange chicken is a staple of Chinese takeout menus across America. This version is packed with orange flavor, thanks to a combo of orange zest and orange juice. Zest the orange first, then squeeze out the juice. Serve over Oven-Baked Rice (page 105).

(see page 84), Oven-Baked Rice (page 105).

INGREDIENTS

2 green onions

1 orange

¾ cup (180 ml) orange juice

4 boneless, skinless chicken breasts (about 2 pounds/900 g)

½ teaspoon salt

3 tablespoons packed brown sugar

2 tablespoons cornstarch

2 tablespoons GF tamari soy sauce

1 tablespoon GF rice vinegar

¼ teaspoon garlic powder

¼ teaspoon ground ginger

2 tablespoons olive oil

TOOLS

Measuring spoons	Liquid measuring cup
Cutting board	2 medium bowls
Chef's knife	Large spoon
2 small bowls	Whisk
Microplane grater or box grater	Large skillet
	Tongs or spatula
Citrus juicer, optional but recommended	

DO THE PREP

1 Rinse the green onions. Lay them on the cutting board and use the chef's knife to cut off the root ends and slice the green onions into thin coins. Set the green onion coins aside in one of the small bowls.

2 Wash the orange. Use the Microplane grater or box grater to zest the orange into the other small bowl. (You'll make the sauce in this bowl later.)

3 On the cutting board, use the chef's knife to cut the zested orange in half at its equator. One at a time, put an orange half in the citrus juicer and squeeze out the juice into the liquid measuring cup. (If you don't have a citrus juicer, use your hand to squeeze the orange, cut side down, until the juice comes out.) Add bottled orange juice to make ¾ cup (180 ml).

4 On the cutting board, use the chef's knife to cut each chicken breast into ½- to 1-inch (13 mm to 2.5 cm) strips, then rotate the strips and slice them into ½- to 1-inch (13 mm to 2.5 cm) cubes. Place the chicken in a medium bowl. Wash your hands!

5 Sprinkle the salt on the chicken and stir with the spoon.

MAKE THE SAUCE

6 Add the orange juice, brown sugar, cornstarch, tamari, rice vinegar, garlic powder, and ginger to the orange zest. Whisk to combine.

DINNER

COOK THE CHICKEN AND SAUCE

7 Heat the skillet on the stovetop over medium-high heat for 1 to 2 minutes, until a drop of water sizzles when you drop it in the skillet (see page 117).

8 Add 1 tablespoon of the oil then use tongs or a spatula to place half of the chicken in the skillet in a single layer. Leave the chicken to cook until it begins to brown on the bottom, about 3 minutes. Stir with the tongs or spatula, then let it cook until most of the liquid has evaporated, 2 to 3 minutes more.

9 When the chicken is completely white and cooked through, use clean tongs or a clean spatula to remove it from the skillet to a clean medium bowl and set it aside.

10 Repeat step 8 with the second tablespoon of oil and the remaining chicken. Leave the second batch of chicken in the skillet when it's cooked.

11 Add the first batch of cooked chicken back to the skillet and pour the sauce over it. Cook, stirring occasionally with the clean tongs or spatula, until the sauce thickens, about 2 minutes. Turn off the heat. Stir in the green onions and serve hot.

CHEF TIP

Make sure to keep food safety in mind. Use one set of tongs or spatula for the raw chicken, and different tongs or spatula for handling the cooked chicken after each batch. No cross-contamination!

AMERICAN GOULASH

MAKES: 6 servings   **PREP TIME:** 15 minutes   **COOK TIME:** 55 minutes

Don't confuse this dish with Hungarian goulash, a thick stew of meat and vegetables that's the national dish of Hungary. This is *American* goulash, with a tomato-based sauce, macaroni-style pasta, and Italian herbs. It is also sometimes known as slumgullion, a term dating back to the California Gold Rush in the 1800s. Try saying *that* word five times fast!

INGREDIENTS

1 large onion

1 green bell pepper

One 28-ounce can (794 g) crushed tomatoes

1 tablespoon olive oil

1 pound (450 g) ground turkey

1 teaspoon garlic powder

1 teaspoon salt

1 quart (1 L) water

2 tablespoons GF Worcestershire sauce

1 teaspoon dried basil

1 teaspoon dried oregano

1 teaspoon sugar

2 cups (280 g) short GF macaroni pasta (like elbows)

1 cup (112 g) shredded cheddar, optional

TOOLS

Can opener

Measuring spoons

Digital kitchen scale or measuring cups

Chef's knife (see Knives, page 8)

Cutting board

Medium bowl

Large saucepan with lid

Spatula

Oven mitts

DO THE PREP

1 Dice the onion using the chef's knife and cutting board. (For instructions on how to dice the onion and a helpful picture, see Red Lentil Dal, page 72.) Place the diced onions in the medium bowl.

2 Rinse the green bell pepper. Place it on its side on the cutting board. Cut a small slice off the top and bottom of the pepper. Stand the pepper up on the cut bottom, then cut the pepper in half. Remove all the seeds and membranes from each half, then lay them on the cutting board skin side down. Slice each half, and the cut-off bottom, into strips about ½ inch (13 mm) wide. Rotate the strips and cut them into squares (see page 73). Add to the onions.

3 Use the can opener to open the can of tomatoes.

COOK THE INGREDIENTS

4 Heat the oil in the saucepan on the stovetop over medium-high heat for about 30 seconds. Add the onions and peppers and cook, stirring occasionally with the spatula, until they begin to soften, about 5 minutes.

5 Add the turkey, garlic powder, and salt. Break up the meat with the spatula. Cook, stirring every few minutes, until the meat is no longer pink and most of the liquid has evaporated, 8 to 10 minutes.

6 Add the water, tomatoes, Worcestershire sauce, basil, oregano, and sugar. Stir with the spatula and bring to a simmer. Turn the heat down to medium-low, place the lid on slightly askew, and simmer for 10 minutes.

7 Remove the lid. Add the pasta and simmer, uncovered, until the pasta is soft, 25 to 30 minutes. Stir the noodles every few minutes to prevent them from sticking together.

FINISH AND ENJOY

8 Serve hot, with shredded cheddar if you'd like.

DINNER

89

GOLDEN PORK CUTLETS

MAKES: 4 to 6 servings   **PREP TIME:** 15 minutes   **COOK TIME:** 20 minutes

Call them whatever you like: breaded pork cutlets (in American English), *cotoletta di maiale alla milanese* (in Italian), or tonkatsu (in Japanese). We call 'em tasty! Their golden color and oh-so-yummy flavor come from using gluten-free corn cereal to make the fine crumbs that coat the pork slices. The end result? A crispy coating, juicy meat, and pleasantly salty flavor that will have you coming back for more. Serve with a side of Roasted Potatoes (page 106) and a salad from the Crunchy Crouton Salad Bar (page 112).

INGREDIENTS

¼ cup (32 g) cornstarch

2 large eggs

½ teaspoon salt

1¾ cups (88 g) GF corn cereal

Eight ¼-inch/6 mm thick
   pork loin cutlets
   (about 1½ pounds/680 g)

Olive oil

TOOLS

Digital kitchen scale or
   measuring cups

Measuring spoons

3 shallow bowls

2 forks

Food processor or blender

Large plate

Wire rack

Large skillet

Tongs

CHEF TIP
If you need to crush cereal but don't have a food processor or blender, put the cereal in a heavy zip-top bag and crush the cereal as small as possible using a heavy skillet, rolling pin, or meat mallet.

DO THE PREP

1 Set three shallow bowls in a row on the kitchen counter or table. Place the cornstarch in the first bowl. Add the eggs and salt to the second bowl, then whisk the eggs with a fork until completely uniform.

2 Use the food processor to grind the cereal into very fine crumbs, almost a powder (see Tip). Add the cereal crumbs to the third bowl.

3 If the pork loin has any tough fat around the edges, use the chef's knife on the cutting board to trim it off.

BREAD THE PORK

4 Working with one pork cutlet at a time, use one of your hands to dip both sides in the cornstarch to coat it completely. Shake off any excess cornstarch.

5 Use your other hand to dip both sides in the egg mixture, coating it so you can't see any cornstarch. Allow any excess egg to drip back into the bowl.

6 Finally, with your cornstarch hand, evenly coat it with the crumbs in the third bowl.

7 Set the coated cutlets aside on a plate. Repeat with the remaining pieces of pork until they're all coated. Wash your hands!

COOK THE PORK

8 Set out the wire rack.

9 Heat the skillet on the stovetop over medium-high heat for 1 to 2 minutes, until a drop of water sizzles when you drop it on the skillet (see page 117). Pour in enough oil to cover the bottom of the skillet with a thin layer.

10 With the fork, place 4 of the breaded cutlets in the skillet. Leave them to cook until the bottoms are golden brown, about 4 minutes. (If your skillet doesn't comfortably fit 4 cutlets at one time, cook the cutlets in smaller batches, adding additional oil to the skillet if needed between batches.) Flip the cutlets with the fork and cook on the second side until both sides are golden brown and the cutlets are cooked through, 4 minutes more. (If you cut one of the cooked cutlets in half, the interior should be completely white, without any pink.)

11 Use the tongs to remove the cooked pork cutlets from the skillet and place them on the wire rack. (Make sure you use clean tongs that haven't touched raw pork. Food safety first!)

12 Repeat steps 10 and 11 until all of the cutlets are cooked. Serve warm.

SPAGHETTI AND MINI MEATBALLS IN EASY MARINARA

MAKES: 4 servings PREP TIME: 20 minutes COOK TIME: 30 minutes

Spaghetti and meatballs with marinara sauce are a beloved Italian American classic. This version uses traditional methods and gluten-free ingredients to make bite-size meatballs that are slow-simmered in a simple marinara sauce. The sauce and meatballs get tossed with your favorite GF spaghetti in a dish that always satisfies. Finish with an extra grating of Parmesan cheese if you like!

INGREDIENTS

MEATBALLS

1 slice GF sandwich bread

1 tablespoon milk

1 large egg

1 tablespoon grated Parmesan

¾ teaspoon dried basil

¾ teaspoon dried oregano

¾ teaspoon salt

½ teaspoon garlic powder

½ teaspoon onion powder

¼ pound (114 g) ground beef

¼ pound (114 g) ground pork

EASY MARINARA SAUCE

One 29-ounce (822 g) can tomato sauce

1 teaspoon dried basil

1 teaspoon dried oregano

1 teaspoon sugar

SPAGHETTI

3 quarts (3 L) water

1 tablespoon salt

12 ounces (340 g) GF spaghetti

TOOLS

Measuring spoons

Digital kitchen scale or measuring cups

Can opener

Food processor

Large bowl

Large spoon

Large plate

Medium saucepan with lid

Tongs

Large saucepan

Colander

PREPARE THE MEATBALLS

1 Pulse the bread in the food processor until it's broken up into small crumbs. If you don't have a food processor, tear the bread into tiny pieces with your fingers. Transfer the bread crumbs to the large bowl. Add the milk. Stir the mixture with the spoon until the bread has absorbed all the milk.

2 Add the egg, Parmesan, basil, oregano, salt, garlic powder, and onion powder to the bread mixture and stir until completely mixed. Add the ground beef and pork and use your hands to mix until everything is combined.

3 Pinch off a small amount of meat mixture, about the size of a grape, roll it into a meatball between your palms, and set it aside on the plate. Repeat to make about 25 meatballs. Wash your hands!

MAKE THE MARINARA SAUCE AND COOK THE MEATBALLS

4 Use the can opener to open the can of tomato sauce. Add the tomato sauce, basil, oregano, and sugar to the medium saucepan, and stir well with the spoon.

5 Using the tongs, add the meatballs to the sauce. Place the saucepan on the stovetop over medium-high heat and bring the sauce to a simmer. Cover with the lid, turn the heat down to medium-low, and simmer for about 30 minutes. Stir the sauce occasionally to prevent it from sticking to the bottom of the saucepan. The sauce is done when the meatballs are cooked through. (Take one out with the spoon and cut it in half; it should be brown all the way through, with no pink.)

BOIL WATER FOR THE SPAGHETTI

6 While you start cooking the meatballs, add the water and salt to the large saucepan and bring it to a boil on the stovetop over high heat.

COOK THE SPAGHETTI

7 When the meatballs have cooked for about 15 minutes, add the spaghetti to the boiling water and cook until it's al dente (see Baked Mac and Cheese, page 42). Stir the spaghetti occasionally to prevent it from sticking together.

FINISH AND ENJOY

8 When the spaghetti is done, place a colander in the sink. Carefully pour the water and cooked spaghetti into the colander to drain.

9 Return the drained spaghetti to the empty saucepan. Add the sauce and meatballs. Stir to combine, then serve hot.

TACO BEEF

Tacos come in all shapes and sizes, from simple to complex, with fillings that range from meat to veggies, beans, and gluten-free grains. You can't go wrong using this easy-but-flavorful beef, complete with a custom spice blend that'll have you coming back for *uno mas* ("one more"). Serve with your favorite taco fixin's: hard or soft GF corn tortillas, shredded cheese, salsa, shredded lettuce—you name it!

INGREDIENTS

1 pound (450 g) ground beef

2 teaspoons chili powder

2 teaspoons ground cumin

¼ teaspoon garlic powder

¼ teaspoon onion powder

¼ teaspoon salt

½ cup (120 ml) water

TOOLS

Measuring spoons

Digital kitchen scale or measuring cups

Large skillet

Spatula

COOK THE MEAT

1 Heat the skillet on the stovetop over medium-high heat for 1 to 2 minutes, until a drop of water sizzles when you drop it in the skillet (see page 117).

2 Add the ground beef and break it into pieces with the spatula. Leave the meat to cook until it starts to brown on the bottom, about 2 minutes. Stir, then leave it to cook for 2 minutes more. Stir again, then cook until the meat is completely brown and the liquid has evaporated from the skillet, about 2 minutes more.

SEASON AND FINISH THE MEAT

3 Add the chili powder, cumin, garlic powder, onion powder, and salt. Stir and cook for 1 minute, until the spices are fragrant.

4 Add the water and cook, stirring occasionally until it evaporates, about 2 minutes. Turn off the heat. Serve hot.

DINNER

95

HAMBURGER SLIDERS

MAKES: 6 sliders **PREP TIME:** 15 minutes **COOK TIME:** 25 minutes

You don't need a flaming backyard grill to make amazing burgers. Many diners and a number of popular fast-casual burger chains use a flattop grill (a flat metal cooking surface) to make their hamburgers and cheeseburgers. For these pint-size sliders, we substitute a large skillet and make our own "tiny buns," since store-bought GF hamburger buns are too big. But the result is the same: burger awesomeness.

INGREDIENTS

BURGERS AND "BUNS"

1 pound (450 g) lean ground beef

12 slices GF sandwich bread

4 tablespoons (½ stick) unsalted butter, melted (see page 12)

1 tablespoon olive oil

½ teaspoon salt

6 slices American, cheddar, or Swiss cheese, optional

BURGER SAUCE

2 tablespoons mayonnaise

1 tablespoon dill relish

1 teaspoon Dijon mustard

1 teaspoon ketchup

¼ teaspoon garlic powder

¼ teaspoon onion powder

¼ teaspoon GF Worcestershire sauce

TOPPINGS

1 large tomato

1 small red onion

Lettuce leaves

TOOLS

Digital kitchen scale or measuring cups

Measuring spoons

Baking sheet

Cutting board

Pint jar lid or 3-inch (7.5 cm) round cookie cutter

Small bowl

Spoon

Chef's knife (see Knives, page 8)

Platter

Salad spinner or 2 clean kitchen towels

Large skillet

Basting brush

Spatula

Large plate

DO THE PREP

1 Divide the meat into 6 equal parts. Roll each into a ball, then flatten into a thin patty about 4 inches (10 cm) wide. Place the patties on the baking sheet and leave at room temperature to warm up a little while you finish preparing the other ingredients. Wash your hands!

2 Lay out the bread slices on the cutting board and use the pint jar lid or 3-inch (7.5 cm) round cutter to cut a round from each slice. Set the rounds aside (it's OK to stack them).

3 In the small bowl, make the sauce by stirring together the mayonnaise, relish, mustard, ketchup, garlic powder, onion powder, and Worcestershire sauce.

4 Wash the tomato. Use the cutting board and chef's knife to cut it into 6 thin slices. Place the tomato slices on the platter.

5 Peel the papery skin off the onion, then cut the top (shoot end) off and cut a few thin slices. Add the onion slices to the platter.

6 Wash and dry the lettuce leaves. Place the lettuce on the platter.

COOK THE "BUNS" AND BURGERS

7 Heat the skillet on the stovetop over medium-high heat for 1 to 2 minutes, until a drop of water sizzles when you drop it in the skillet (see page 117).

8 On the cutting board, use the basting brush to brush both sides of each round of bread with butter. Without overlapping, place a few rounds of the buttered bread in the hot skillet. Allow them to toast until golden brown, 10 to 15 seconds. You can lift an edge with the spatula and peek while they're toasting, to make sure they're just right.

9 Flip the bread with the spatula and toast the second side for 10 to 15 seconds more. Use the spatula to remove the toasted bread from the skillet and set aside. Repeat with the rest of the rounds until all the bread is toasted on both sides.

10 Add 1½ teaspoons of the oil to the hot skillet. Using the spatula, carefully place 3 of the burger patties in the skillet. Sprinkle ⅛ teaspoon salt across the tops of the 3 burgers. Cook for about 4 minutes, until charred on the bottom.

CHEF TIP

Save the crusts from the bread to turn into bread crumbs or croutons. Store them in the freezer in an airtight container or heavy zip-top bag until you're ready to use them.

11 Flip the burgers with the spatula and sprinkle the tops with ⅛ teaspoon of the salt. If you're making cheeseburgers, place 1 slice of the cheese on top of each burger now. Cook until the second side is charred on the bottom, 4 minutes more, then use the spatula to remove the burgers from the skillet and place them on the plate.

12 Repeat steps 10 and 11 with the remaining 3 patties.

ASSEMBLE THE BURGERS

13 Place 1 round of toasted bread on a plate, then add the burger, top with a spoonful of sauce, and add any toppings you'd like. Finish with a second round of bread. Repeat with the remaining sliders and serve!

97

SIDES

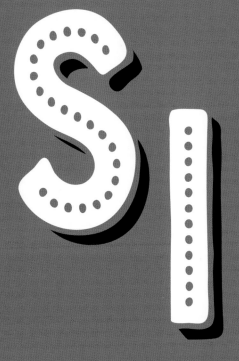

CORNBREAD MUFFINS

MAKES: 12 muffins   PREP TIME: 15 minutes   COOK TIME: 18 to 20 minutes

Eat them plain. Spread them with butter or honey. Pair them with a hot bowl of chili. Use them as the base for Thanksgiving stuffing. Cornbread is great with lots of stuff! And with this recipe, we bet none of your family or friends will guess it's gluten-free.

INGREDIENTS

GF nonstick cooking spray

1 cup (125 g) GF all-purpose flour blend

1 cup (152 g) GF cornmeal

2 tablespoons sugar

1 tablespoon baking powder

1 teaspoon salt

1 cup (240 ml) milk

2 large eggs

6 tablespoons (¾ stick) unsalted butter, melted (see page 12)

TOOLS

Digital kitchen scale or measuring cups

Measuring spoons

Muffin pan

Medium bowl

Whisk

Large cookie scoop or large spoon

Oven mitts

Wire rack

SIDES

DO THE PREP

1 Preheat the oven to 400°F (200°C).

2 Grease the muffin pan cups with cooking spray.

MAKE THE BATTER

3 In the bowl, whisk together the flour, cornmeal, sugar, baking powder, and salt.

4 Add the milk and eggs and whisk to combine.

5 Add the melted butter and whisk until the ingredients are completely mixed.

BAKE THE CORNBREAD

6 Divide the batter evenly among the 12 muffin cups. (Using a large cookie scoop to portion the batter into the cups makes this really easy. Use a spoon if you don't have a cookie scoop.)

7 Put the muffin pan in the oven. Bake for 18 to 20 minutes, until the muffins are golden brown on top or when a wooden toothpick inserted in the center of a muffin comes out clean.

SERVE AND ENJOY

8 Wearing oven mitts, carefully remove the muffin pan from the oven and set aside to cool. When the muffins are cool enough to handle, take them out of the pan to finish cooling directly on the wire rack. Enjoy warm or at room temperature.

BISCUITS

MAKES: 12 biscuits **PREP TIME:** 15 minutes **COOK TIME:** 10 to 12 minutes

These buttery American-style biscuits are light and tender. They're a great side for a wide range of dinners, from chicken noodle soup to dishes with sauces and gravy that you want to sop up!

INGREDIENTS

GF nonstick cooking spray

2½ cups (312 g) GF all-purpose flour blend

1½ tablespoons baking powder

1 tablespoon sugar

¾ teaspoon salt

8 tablespoons (1 stick) unsalted butter, cold

1 cup (240 ml) milk

TOOLS

Digital kitchen scale or measuring cups

Measuring spoons

Baking sheet

Medium bowl

Large spoon

Cutting board

Butter knife

Large cookie scoop or large spoon

Oven mitts

DO THE PREP

1 Preheat the oven to 450°F (230°C).

2 Grease the baking sheet lightly with cooking spray.

MAKE THE DOUGH

3 Add the flour, baking powder, sugar, and salt to the bowl and mix with the spoon.

4 On the cutting board, use the butter knife to cut the butter into small pieces. (Smaller pieces will be easier to work into the flour mixture.)

5 Add the butter to the flour mixture. Use your hands to pinch and squeeze the butter with the other ingredients until it's all mixed together and looks like wet sand.

6 Add the milk and stir with the spoon to form a stiff dough.

BAKE THE BISCUITS

7 Use the large cookie scoop or large spoon to make pieces of dough a little larger than a golf ball. Roll each piece into a ball between your palms and place the balls on the baking sheet about 2 inches (5 cm) apart. Gently flatten the balls to form disks about 1 inch (2.5 cm) tall.

8 Put the baking sheet in the oven. Bake for 10 to 12 minutes, until the biscuits are golden brown on top.

SERVE AND ENJOY

9 Wearing oven mitts, carefully remove the baking sheet from the oven. Allow the biscuits to cool on the baking sheet for a few minutes before serving. Enjoy warm or at room temperature.

SIDES

PAN DE YUCA

MAKES: 20 rolls   **PREP TIME:** 15 minutes   **COOK TIME:** 12 to 13 minutes

Pan de yuca is a naturally gluten-free cheese bread from Latin America. Two especially popular versions hail from Colombia and Brazil in South America. Its two core ingredients—tapioca starch and Mexican queso fresco—combine to make moist, tender, chewy rolls that you'll want to gobble up like candy. They're a fabulous alternative to normal dinner rolls.

INGREDIENTS

10 ounces (285 g) queso fresco

1 cup (160 g) tapioca starch

1 teaspoon baking powder

¼ teaspoon salt

1 large egg

3 tablespoons milk

TOOLS

Digital kitchen scale or measuring cups

Measuring spoons

Butter knife

Food processor

Rubber spatula

Rimmed baking sheet

Oven mitts

DO THE PREP

1 Preheat the oven to 350°F (180°C).

MAKE THE DOUGH

2 Break the cheese into a few pieces and put them in a food processor. Pulse a few times to break the cheese into smaller pieces.

3 Add the tapioca starch, baking powder, and salt and pulse to combine completely.

4 Add the egg and milk. Turn the food processor on and blend just until a dough forms. Turn off the food processor. (Not all the ingredients will be incorporated into the dough ball, but that's OK.)

SHAPE AND BAKE THE ROLLS

5 Remove the food processor bowl from the machine, take off the cover, and take the blade out. Be careful with the food processor blade because it is very sharp. Use the rubber spatula to scrape the dough out of the food processor bowl onto the counter. Squeeze the dough together into one big ball.

6 Roll the dough with your hands into a long "snake" about 16 inches (40.5 cm) long. Use the butter knife to cut the snake in half, then cut each half in half again to get quarters. Cut each quarter in half to make eighths, then cut each piece in half to get sixteen 1-inch (2.5 cm) pieces.

7 Roll each piece of dough between your hands to make a ball. Place the balls about 2 inches (5 cm) apart on the rimmed baking sheet. (They'll spread as they bake.)

8 Put the baking sheet in the oven and bake the rolls for 10 minutes. Then turn the oven to broil. Broil for 2 to 3 minutes, until the tops of the rolls have golden spots. (Watch the rolls carefully so they don't burn!)

SERVE AND ENJOY

9 Wearing oven mitts, carefully remove the baking sheet from the oven. Let the rolls cool for about 5 minutes. Then remove them from the baking sheet and serve warm or at room temperature.

OVEN-BAKED RICE

MAKES: 4 servings **PREP TIME:** 5 minutes **COOK TIME:** 25 minutes

If you're gluten-free, rice is probably one of your best friends at mealtime. It's a great source of carbohydrates, so it gives your body energy. And it tastes delicious as a side dish with almost everything! Lots of rice recipes call for cooking it on the stovetop or in an electric rice cooker, but this one keeps things easy by using the oven to make perfect rice every time.

INGREDIENTS

1¾ cups (420 ml) water

1 cup (208 g) white jasmine rice

1 tablespoon olive oil

1 teaspoon salt

TOOLS

Digital kitchen scale or measuring cups

Measuring spoons

Kettle or small saucepan

1-quart (1 L) baking dish with lid

Large spoon

Oven mitts

Aluminum foil

DO THE PREP

1 Preheat the oven to 375°F (190°C).

2 Add the water to the kettle or saucepan and bring it to a boil on the stovetop over high heat.

MIX AND BAKE THE RICE

3 Add the rice, oil, and salt to the baking dish and stir with the spoon.

4 Carefully add the boiling water, then stir to combine. Cover the baking dish with its lid or cover it tightly with aluminum foil. If you use foil, be careful, since the baking dish will be hot from the boiling water.

BAKE AND SERVE

5 Wearing oven mitts, put the baking dish in the oven. Bake the rice for 25 minutes.

6 Wearing oven mitts, carefully remove the baking dish from the oven and allow the rice to cool for 5 minutes.

7 Wearing oven mitts, carefully remove the lid or aluminum foil. Stir the rice with the spoon to fluff it. Serve hot.

SIDES

105

ROASTED POTATOES

MAKES: 4 servings   **PREP TIME:** 15 minutes   **COOK TIME:** 35 to 40 minutes

Starch is an important part of a balanced meal, and there's no easier way to make it gluten-free than with these simple oven-roasted potatoes. The recipe works equally well for both white and yellow potatoes (like our preferred Yukon Gold), as well as sweet potatoes.

INGREDIENTS

4 medium Yukon Gold or sweet potatoes (about 1½ pounds/680 g)

¼ cup (60 ml) olive oil

½ teaspoon salt

TOOLS

Measuring spoons

Vegetable scrub brush or rough sponge

Cutting board

Chef's knife (see Knives, page 8)

Rimmed baking sheet

Tongs, optional

Oven mitts

Spatula

DO THE PREP

1 Preheat the oven to 400°F (200°C).

2 Wash the potatoes with the scrub brush or rough sponge to clean off any dirt.

3 Dice the potatoes into 1-inch (2.5 cm) cubes using the cutting board and chef's knife:

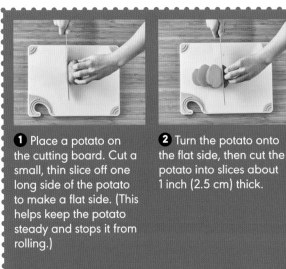

1 Place a potato on the cutting board. Cut a small, thin slice off one long side of the potato to make a flat side. (This helps keep the potato steady and stops it from rolling.)

2 Turn the potato onto the flat side, then cut the potato into slices about 1 inch (2.5 cm) thick.

3 Lay the slices flat and cut them into strips about 1 inch (2.5 cm) wide. Rotate the strips and cut them into 1-inch (2.5 cm) cubes. Repeat with the remaining potatoes.

4 Spread the cubed potatoes on the rimmed baking sheet. Drizzle with the oil and sprinkle with the salt. Toss with your hands or tongs to coat all sides of the potatoes.

BAKE AND SERVE

5 Put the baking sheet in the oven and bake the potato cubes for 20 minutes.

6 Wearing oven mitts, carefully remove the baking sheet from the oven. Toss the potatoes with the spatula. Return the baking sheet to the oven and bake for 15 to 20 minutes more, until the potatoes are golden brown and tender.

7 Wearing oven mitts, carefully remove the baking sheet from the oven. Serve hot.

MASHED POTATOES

MAKES: 4 servings **PREP TIME:** 15 minutes **COOK TIME:** 20 minutes

From normal weeknight dinners like roast chicken with gravy to special occasions like Thanksgiving, making great mashed potatoes is a skill that will serve you well—and make your taste buds happy.

INGREDIENTS

- 4 medium Yukon Gold potatoes (about 1½ pounds/680 g)
- 4 tablespoons (½ stick) unsalted butter
- ½ cup (120 ml) heavy cream
- ½ teaspoon salt
- ¼ teaspoon black pepper

TOOLS

Digital kitchen scale or measuring cups

Measuring spoons

Vegetable peeler

Cutting board

Chef's knife (see Knives, page 8)

Colander

Large saucepan

Fork

Potato masher

Large spoon

PREP THE POTATOES

1 Peel the potatoes with the vegetable peeler. (Compost the potato skins, if you can.)

2 Cut the peeled potatoes on a cutting board, using a chef's knife: Cut each potato in half, then lay the halves flat on their cut side. Slice each half into quarters.

BOIL THE POTATOES

3 Place the potato pieces in the saucepan and completely cover them with cold water.

4 Place the saucepan on the stovetop over high heat and bring to a boil. When the water is boiling, turn the heat down to medium so the water simmers. Cook until the fork can easily pierce the potatoes, about 20 minutes. While the potatoes are cooking, put the colander in the sink.

FINISH AND ENJOY

5 Carefully pour the water and cooked potatoes into the colander to drain. Add the drained potatoes back to the empty saucepan.

6 Use the potato masher to mash the potatoes until almost smooth.

7 Add the butter, then leave the potatoes to rest until the butter is melted, about 2 minutes.

8 Add the heavy cream, salt, and pepper and stir until combined. Serve hot.

SIDES

ROASTED VEGGIES

MAKES: 4 servings **PREP TIME:** 10 minutes **COOK TIME:** 30 minutes

We bet your parents have told you to "eat your veggies." With this recipe, you can enjoy those veggies and make your parents happy at the same time. Forget bland, soggy, steamed vegetables. Take your pick from broccoli, cauliflower, carrots, or beets, and savor them like you never have before!

INGREDIENTS

2 pounds (900 g) vegetables (2 broccoli crowns, 1 large head cauliflower, about 10 carrots, about 6 beets)

¼ cup (60 ml) olive oil

½ teaspoon garlic powder

½ teaspoon salt

TOOLS

Measuring spoons

Chef's knife (see Knives, page 8)

Cutting board

Vegetable peeler

Rimmed baking sheet

Tongs

Oven mitts

DO THE PREP

1 Preheat the oven to 400°F (200°C).

2 Rinse and cut the vegetables into bite-size pieces using the chef's knife and cutting board:

For broccoli and cauliflower, break the crowns into small florets and cut any large ones in half or quarters. (Compost stems and base, if you can.)

For carrots, cut off the tops, peel, and slice the carrots into ½-inch (13 mm) coins.

For beets, cut off the tops, peel, and cut into ½-inch (13 mm) cubes. (See Roasted Potatoes, page 106, for how to cut them into cubes.)

3 Spread the vegetables on the rimmed baking sheet. Drizzle with the oil and sprinkle with the garlic powder and salt. Toss with your hands or tongs to evenly coat the vegetables, then spread them in a single layer.

BAKE AND SERVE

4 Put the baking sheet in the oven and bake for 20 minutes.

5 Wearing oven mitts, carefully remove the baking sheet from the oven. Toss the vegetables with the tongs. Return the baking sheet to the oven for about 10 minutes more, until the vegetables are tender, brown, and crispy in places. Serve hot.

SWEET AND SPICY BRUSSELS SPROUTS

MAKES: 4 servings **PREP TIME:** 15 minutes **COOK TIME:** 30 minutes

Brussels sprouts are named for the capital city of Belgium, where they were first cultivated more than 400 years ago. The sweet-and-spicy glaze makes the tender oven-roasted sprouts as tasty as candy—or at least as close to candy as vegetables can get!

INGREDIENTS

2 pounds (900 g) Brussels sprouts

⅓ cup (80 ml) plus 2 tablespoons olive oil

1 teaspoon garlic powder

¾ teaspoon salt

½ teaspoon black pepper

2 tablespoons agave nectar

2 teaspoons ground fresh chili paste (also called sambal oelek)

TOOLS

Liquid measuring cup

Measuring spoons

Cutting board

Chef's knife (see Knives, page 8)

Rimmed baking sheet

Oven mitts

Tongs

Serving bowl or plate

Small bowl

Spoon

DO THE PREP

1 Preheat the oven to 400°F (200°C).

2 Rinse the Brussels sprouts. On the cutting board, use the chef's knife to cut the bottom off each sprout, then cut the larger sprouts into quarters and the smaller sprouts into halves. You want bite-size pieces, all about the same size.

BAKE THE SPROUTS

3 Spread the Brussels sprout pieces on the rimmed baking sheet. Drizzle them with ⅓ cup (80 ml) of the oil. Sprinkle with the garlic powder, salt, and pepper. Toss everything together with your hands or tongs and spread in an even layer on the baking sheet.

4 Put the baking sheet in the oven and bake the Brussels sprouts for 20 minutes.

5 Wearing oven mitts, carefully remove the baking sheet from the oven. Drizzle the Brussels sprouts with the remaining 2 tablespoons oil and toss them with the tongs. Return the baking sheet to the oven for 10 minutes more, until the Brussels sprouts are tender and well-charred.

DRIZZLE WITH THE SAUCE AND SERVE

6 Use the tongs to transfer the Brussels sprouts to the serving bowl or plate.

7 In the small bowl, stir together the agave nectar and chili paste. Drizzle over the Brussels sprouts and toss with the tongs to coat. Serve hot.

CRUNCHY CROUTON SALAD BAR

Salads are often naturally gluten-free . . . unless they're topped with pesky croutons made from wheat bread. With this recipe, you can enjoy that same satisfying crunch on your salads. You'll find recipes below for five flavorful dressings to finish off any salad bowl, as well as suggestions for the best salad ingredients to use for each one.

CROUTONS

MAKES: 4 servings **PREP TIME:** 5 minutes
COOK TIME: 15 minutes

INGREDIENTS

4 slices GF sandwich bread

2 tablespoons olive oil

¼ teaspoon garlic powder

⅛ teaspoon salt

TOOLS

Measuring spoons

Cutting board

Serrated knife (see Knives, page 8)

Rimmed baking sheet

Tongs

Oven mitts

DO THE PREP

1 Preheat the oven to 375°F (190°C).

2 On the cutting board, use the serrated knife to cut the bread into ½-inch (13 mm) cubes. Place the bread cubes on the rimmed baking sheet.

3 Drizzle the bread cubes with the oil and sprinkle with the garlic powder and salt. Toss everything together with your hands or tongs to evenly coat.

BAKE AND SERVE

4 Put the baking sheet in the oven. Bake for 8 to 10 minutes, until the bread begins to turn brown. Wearing oven mitts, carefully remove the baking sheet from the oven.

5 Toss the croutons with the tongs. Return the baking sheet to the oven for 3 to 5 minutes more, until the croutons are golden brown and crispy.

6 Wearing oven mitts, carefully remove the baking sheet from the oven and allow it to cool completely. Add the croutons to any salad, or store in an airtight container at room temperature for up to 4 days.

STRAWBERRY BALSAMIC DRESSING

MAKES: about ½ cup (120 ml) dressing (about 4 servings)
PREP TIME: 5 minutes (for the dressing only)

INGREDIENTS

1 cup (150 g) chopped fresh strawberries

2 tablespoons balsamic vinegar

¼ cup (60 ml) olive oil

⅛ teaspoon salt

⅛ teaspoon black pepper

SUGGESTED SALAD

Spinach

Diced avocado

Chopped pecans

TOOLS

Digital kitchen scale or measuring cups

Measuring spoons

Blender

Large bowl

Tongs

Add the strawberries, balsamic vinegar, oil, salt, and pepper to the blender and puree until smooth. Pour over the salad ingredients in a large bowl and toss everything with the tongs.

SIDES

113

EASY CAESAR DRESSING

MAKES: about ½ cup (120 ml) dressing (about 4 servings)
PREP TIME: 5 minutes (for the dressing only)

INGREDIENTS

½ lemon (about 1 tablespoon juice)

¼ cup (60 ml) olive oil

2 tablespoons grated Parmesan

1 tablespoon Dijon mustard

2 teaspoons prepared horseradish

½ teaspoon GF Worcestershire sauce

SUGGESTED SALAD

Chopped romaine lettuce

TOOLS

Liquid measuring cup

Measuring spoons

Citrus juicer, optional but recommended

Large bowl

Whisk

Tongs

1 Put the lemon half in the citrus juicer and squeeze out the juice into the bowl. (If you don't have a citrus juicer, you can use your hand to squeeze the lemon, cut side down, until the juice comes out.)

2 Add the oil, Parmesan, mustard, horseradish, and Worcestershire sauce. Whisk everything together until uniformly mixed.

3 Add the lettuce and toss with the tongs to coat it.

HONEY MUSTARD DRESSING

MAKES: about ½ cup (120 ml) dressing (about 4 servings)
PREP TIME: 5 minutes (for the dressing only)

INGREDIENTS

½ lemon (about 1 tablespoon juice)

2 tablespoons Dijon mustard

2 tablespoons honey

2 tablespoons olive oil

SUGGESTED SALAD

Chopped green leaf or red leaf lettuce

Green apple, thinly sliced

Chopped pecans

TOOLS

Measuring spoons

Citrus juicer, optional but recommended

Large bowl

Whisk

Tongs

1 Put the lemon half in the citrus juicer and squeeze out the juice into the bowl.

2 Add the mustard, honey and oil, and whisk everything together until uniformly mixed.

3 Add the salad ingredients and toss with the tongs to coat everything.

LEMON VINAIGRETTE

MAKES: about 1/3 cup (80 ml) dressing (about 4 servings)

PREP TIME: 5 minutes (for the dressing only)

INGREDIENTS

- ½ lemon (about 1 tablespoon juice)
- ¼ cup (60 ml) olive oil
- ½ teaspoon Dijon mustard
- ⅛ teaspoon garlic powder
- ⅛ teaspoon salt
- ⅛ teaspoon black pepper

SUGGESTED SALAD

- Chopped green leaf or red leaf lettuce
- Crumbled feta
- Grape tomatoes
- Sliced cucumber

TOOLS

- Liquid measuring cup
- Measuring spoons
- Citrus juicer, optional but recommended
- Large bowl
- Whisk
- Tongs

1 Put the lemon half in the citrus juicer and squeeze out the juice into the bowl. (If you don't have a citrus juicer, you can squeeze the lemon, cut side down, with your hand until the juice comes out.)

2 Add the oil, mustard, garlic powder, salt, and pepper. Whisk everything together until uniformly mixed.

3 Add the salad ingredients and toss with the tongs to coat everything.

CHEF TIP
Put the unused half of a lemon in a sealed small container to use for another recipe. It will keep for up to 4 days in the refrigerator.

SESAME-SOY DRESSING

MAKES: about ½ cup (120 ml) dressing (about 4 servings)

PREP TIME: 5 minutes (for the dressing only)

INGREDIENTS

- 2 tablespoons GF rice vinegar
- 2 tablespoons olive oil
- 2 tablespoons GF tamari soy sauce
- 1 tablespoon packed brown sugar
- 1 teaspoon sesame oil

SUGGESTED SALAD

- Chopped romaine
- Sliced red bell pepper
- Mandarin oranges

TOOLS

- Measuring spoons
- Large bowl
- Whisk
- Tongs

In the large bowl, whisk together the rice vinegar, olive oil, tamari, brown sugar, and sesame oil until uniformly mixed. Add the salad ingredients and toss with the tongs to coat everything.

SIDES

BLISTERED SHISHITOS

MAKES: 4 servings   PREP TIME: 5 minutes   COOK TIME: 10 minutes

Shishito peppers are native to East Asia, including the countries Japan and Korea. They're usually mild and sweet, but every now and then, you get a spicy one as a surprise. When they're blistered and blackened in a skillet, then tossed in a bit of lime juice and salt, it's easy to eat them rapid-fire like potato chips or strawberries!

INGREDIENTS

24 shishito peppers (about 8 ounces/ 227 g)

1 tablespoon olive oil

½ lime (about 1 tablespoon juice)

⅛ teaspoon salt

TOOLS

Measuring spoons

Kitchen towel

Large skillet

Tongs

Serving bowl

Citrus juicer, optional but recommended

DO THE PREP

1 Rinse the shishitos. Spread them out on a kitchen towel and dry them to remove any excess water that could splatter in the skillet.

2 Heat the skillet on the stovetop over medium-high heat for 1 to 2 minutes, until a small drop of water sizzles when you drop it in the skillet (see Tip).

BLISTER THE PEPPERS

3 When the skillet is hot, add the oil, then the shishitos. Be careful, since the oil can "pop" a little when you add the peppers.

4 Cook for about 10 minutes, turning with tongs every 2 minutes, until the shishitos are charred on all sides and very soft. Remove the skillet from the heat.

SERVE AND ENJOY

5 Use the tongs to move the shishitos from the skillet to the bowl.

CHEF TIP
You know your pan is hot when a small drop of water sizzles.

6 Put the lime half in the citrus juicer and squeeze out the juice over the shishitos. (If you don't have a citrus juicer, you can use your hand to squeeze the lime, cut side down, until the juice comes out.)

7 Sprinkle the shishitos with the salt. Toss with the tongs to coat evenly and serve warm.

DESSERT

APPLE BARS

MAKES: 9 servings PREP TIME: 20 minutes COOK TIME: 70 minutes

These amazing apple bars have all the flavors of apple pie without the need to make pastry dough and roll out a pie shell! They start with a simple pressed crust. Next, a layer of mildly sweet apple filling follows. Finally, they're capped with a light streusel (crumble) topping and a little sweet icing that will have you licking your lips.

INGREDIENTS

GF nonstick cooking spray

BASE AND STREUSEL

2 cups (250 g) GF all-purpose flour blend*

1 cup (200 g) sugar

1 teaspoon xanthan gum

½ teaspoon ground cinnamon

½ teaspoon salt

12 tablespoons (1½ sticks) unsalted butter, cold

FILLING

6 to 8 apples (about 2½ pounds/1.1 kg)

2 lemons (about ⅓ cup/80 ml juice)

½ cup (100 g) granulated sugar

1 teaspoon ground cinnamon

¼ teaspoon ground nutmeg

ICING

½ cup (60 g) confectioners' sugar

2 teaspoons milk

TOOLS

Digital kitchen scale or measuring cups

Measuring spoons

9-inch (23 cm) square baking pan

Large bowl

Large spoon

Cutting board

Butter knife

Small bowl

Oven mitts

Vegetable peeler

Apple cutter (or chef's knife)

Medium saucepan with lid

Citrus juicer, optional but recommended

Oven mitts

Potato masher

Small zip-top plastic bag

DO THE PREP

1 Preheat the oven to 375°F (190°C).

2 Grease the baking pan with cooking spray.

MAKE THE BASE AND STREUSEL

3 Add the flour, granulated sugar, xanthan gum, cinnamon, and salt to the large bowl. Stir with the spoon to combine.

4 On the cutting board, use the butter knife to cut the butter into small pieces. (Smaller pieces will be easier to work into the flour mixture.)

5 Add the butter to the flour mixture. Use your fingers to pinch and squeeze the butter with the other ingredients until it's all mixed together and looks like small crumbles. (For a helpful picture, see Biscuits, page 103.)

6 Set aside 1 cup (150 g) of the streusel mixture in the small bowl. Press the remaining mixture into the bottom of the prepared baking pan to make an even, firm layer of crust.

*High-altitude adjustment: Use 2¼ cups (281 g) GF all-purpose flour blend.

7 Put the baking pan in the oven. Bake the crust for 10 minutes, just until it begins to bubble around the edges. (It won't change color much.)

8 Wearing oven mitts, carefully remove the baking pan from the oven and set it aside to cool.

MAKE THE FILLING

9 Peel the apples with the vegetable peeler. Core and slice the peeled apples with an apple cutter. (If you don't have an apple cutter, put the apples on the cutting board and use the chef's knife to cut each apple into 8 wedges. Cut out the core from each wedge. Ask an adult for help if you need to.) Place the apples in the saucepan.

10 On the cutting board, use the chef's knife to cut the lemons in half at their equators. One at a time, put a lemon half in the citrus juicer and squeeze out the juice over the apples. (If you don't have a citrus juicer, use your hand to squeeze the lemons, cut side down, until the juice comes out.)

11 Add the sugar, cinnamon, and nutmeg to the apples and stir.

12 Cover the saucepan with its lid and place it on the stovetop over medium heat. Cook until the apples are very tender, about 20 minutes, stirring about every 5 minutes. Turn off the heat and move the saucepan to a cool burner.

13 Use the potato masher to break the apples into smaller pieces.

14 Using the spoon, carefully spread the hot apple filling over the baked crust. Sprinkle the reserved streusel crumbles evenly on top. Bake for 40 minutes more, until the apple bars are golden brown.

15 Wearing oven mitts, carefully remove the baking pan from the oven and set it aside to cool.

MAKE THE ICING

16 While the bars are cooling, add the confectioners' sugar and milk to the small bowl and stir to combine. Put the icing in the zip-top bag.

17 After the bars have cooled for about 10 minutes, cut a small corner off of the bag and drizzle the icing over the top in decorative lines. Serve warm or at room temperature.

DESSERT

BLUEBERRY COBBLER

MAKES: 8 servings **PREP TIME:** 15 minutes **COOK TIME:** 20 minutes

Made with your choice of fresh or frozen blueberries, this cobbler is topped with a buttery, tender dough that perfectly complements the sweet berries. Serve with a scoop of vanilla ice cream or a dollop of whipped cream.

INGREDIENTS

FILLING

- ½ cup (100 g) sugar
- ¼ cup (60 ml) water
- 2 tablespoons cornstarch
- 4 cups (580 g) fresh or frozen blueberries
- ½ lemon (about 1 tablespoon juice)

TOPPING

- 1 cup (125 g) GF all-purpose flour blend
- 2 tablespoons sugar
- 1½ teaspoons baking powder
- ¼ teaspoon salt
- 4 tablespoons (½ stick) unsalted butter, cold
- ¼ cup (60 ml) milk
- 1 large egg
- 1 teaspoon GF pure vanilla extract

TOOLS

- Digital kitchen scale or measuring cups
- Measuring spoons
- Medium saucepan
- Large spoon
- Citrus juicer, optional but recommended
- Medium bowl
- Cutting board
- Butter knife
- Small bowl
- 2-quart (2 L) baking dish or 9-inch (23 cm) square baking pan
- Toothpick
- Oven mitts

DO THE PREP

1 Preheat the oven to 400°F (200°C).

MAKE THE FILLING

2 Add the sugar, water, and cornstarch to the saucepan and stir to combine.

3 Add the blueberries. Bring to a boil on the stovetop over medium-high heat, stirring constantly. Cook until the blueberry mixture thickens, about 5 minutes. Turn off the heat and move the saucepan to a cool burner.

4 Place the lemon half in the citrus juicer and squeeze out the juice over the blueberries. (If you don't have a citrus juicer, you can use your hand to squeeze the lemon, cut side down, until the juice comes out.) Stir, then leave to cool.

DESSERT

122

MAKE THE TOPPING

5 Add the flour, sugar, baking powder, and salt to the medium bowl. Stir to combine.

6 On the cutting board, use the butter knife to cut the butter into small pieces. (Smaller pieces will be easier to work into the flour mixture.)

7 Add the butter to the flour mixture and use your hands to pinch and squeeze the butter with the flour until it's all mixed together and looks like small crumbles. (For a helpful picture, see Biscuits, page 103.)

8 In the small bowl, whisk together the milk, egg, and vanilla.

9 Add the milk mixture to the flour-butter mixture and stir to combine.

BAKE THE COBBLER

10 Pour the blueberry filling into the baking dish. Spoon the topping over the filling in 8 dollops.

11 Put the baking dish in the oven. Bake for 20 minutes, until the topping is golden brown and a toothpick inserted in one of the topping dollops comes out mostly clean. (A few little crumbs on the toothpick are OK.)

12 Wearing oven mitts, carefully remove the baking dish from the oven. Allow it to cool for a few minutes before serving. Serve warm or at room temperature.

CONFETTI CUPCAKES WITH VANILLA FROSTING

MAKES: 12 cupcakes **PREP TIME:** 15 minutes **COOK TIME:** 25 minutes **DECORATE TIME:** 15 minutes

Nothing says "fun" quite like confetti cupcakes—vanilla cupcakes studded with bright multicolored rainbow sprinkles and topped with vanilla frosting and more sprinkles. Planning a birthday treat? Look no further!

INGREDIENTS

CUPCAKES

- ¾ cup (150 g) granulated sugar
- 8 tablespoons (1 stick) unsalted butter, room temperature (see page 12)
- 2 teaspoons GF pure vanilla extract
- 1 large egg
- 2 large egg whites (see page 12; discard the yolks)
- ½ cup (120 ml) milk
- ¼ cup (60 g) sour cream
- 1½ cups (188 g) GF all-purpose flour blend*
- 1½ teaspoons baking powder
- 1 teaspoon xanthan gum
- ½ teaspoon baking soda
- ½ teaspoon salt
- ⅓ cup (64 g) rainbow sprinkles

FROSTING AND TOPPING

- 8 tablespoons (1 stick) unsalted butter, room temperature (take it out of the refrigerator when you turn the oven on)
- 2 cups (240 g) confectioners' sugar
- 1 teaspoon GF pure vanilla extract
- 2 tablespoons milk
- ¼ teaspoon salt
- ½ cup (96 g) rainbow sprinkles

*High-altitude adjustment: Use 1¾ cups (219 g) GF all-purpose flour blend.

TOOLS

- Digital kitchen scale or measuring cups
- Measuring spoons
- Muffin pan
- 12 cupcake liners
- Stand mixer, or handheld mixer and large bowl
- Rubber spatula
- Small bowl
- Whisk
- Large cookie or ice cream scoop, or large spoon
- Toothpick
- Oven mitts
- Wire rack
- Palette knife or butter knife

DO THE PREP

1 Preheat the oven to 350°F (180°C).

2 Line the 12 cups of a muffin pan with cupcake liners.

MAKE THE CUPCAKE BATTER

3 Add the granulated sugar, butter, and vanilla to the bowl of the stand mixer, or a large bowl if you're using a handheld mixer. Mix at medium speed until light and fluffy, about 2 minutes.

4 Stop the mixer and scrape down the sides of the bowl with the rubber spatula. Add the egg and egg whites and mix on low speed to incorporate them.

5 Add the milk and sour cream and mix just until combined. (The mixture will be very thin and liquidy.)

6 In the small bowl, whisk together the flour, baking powder, xanthan gum, baking soda, and salt.

7 Add the flour mixture to the liquid mixture and mix on low speed to combine, about 10 seconds.

8 Stop the mixer and scrape down the sides of the bowl with the rubber spatula. Add the ⅓ cup (64 g) sprinkles, then mix on high speed until the batter is smooth and completely mixed, about 5 seconds.

BAKE THE CUPCAKES

9 Scoop and divide the batter among the 12 cupcake liners, leaving the top as smooth as possible. (Using a large cookie or ice cream scoop makes this task easier, but a spoon will also work.) Wash and dry the bowl and beaters.

10 Put the muffin pan in the oven. Bake for 25 minutes, until the cupcakes are golden brown on top and a toothpick inserted into the center of a cupcake comes out mostly clean. (A few little crumbs on the toothpick are OK.)

CHEF TIP
Use an ice cream scoop or a spoon to divide your batter.

11 Wearing oven mitts, carefully remove the muffin pan from the oven and set aside to cool for a few minutes.

12 When the cupcakes are cool enough to touch, take them out of the pan and place them on the wire rack. Allow them to cool to room temperature.

MAKE THE FROSTING AND DECORATE

13 Add the butter to the bowl of the stand mixer, or the medium bowl if you're using a handheld mixer. Mix on medium-high until smooth, about 1 minute.

14 Add the confectioners' sugar, vanilla, milk, and salt and mix on medium-high speed until smooth and fluffy, about 3 minutes. If the frosting is too thick to spread easily, add additional milk, 1 teaspoon at a time, until it is the right consistency for spreading.

15 Place the ½ cup (96 g) rainbow sprinkles in the small bowl.

16 Frost one cupcake at a time with the palette knife or butter knife. Dip the top of each cupcake into the bowl of sprinkles as you go. Repeat with the rest of the cupcakes. Enjoy!

CHOCOLATE CAKE WITH CHOCOLATE FROSTING

MAKES: one 2-layer 8- or 9-inch (20 or 23 cm) cake **PREP TIME:** 15 minutes
COOK TIME: 40 to 45 minutes **DECORATE TIME:** 15 minutes

What goes best with chocolate? More chocolate! This recipe is a chocolate lover's dream: two layers of moist chocolate cake slathered with rich chocolate frosting.

INGREDIENTS

CAKE

GF nonstick cooking spray

2¼ cups (281 g) GF all-purpose flour blend*

2 teaspoons baking powder

1 teaspoon xanthan gum

1 teaspoon baking soda

1 teaspoon salt

2 cups (400 g) granulated sugar

1 cup (240 ml) milk

¾ cup (72 g) cocoa powder

½ cup (120 ml) vegetable oil

2 large eggs

2 teaspoons GF pure vanilla extract

1 cup (240 ml) hot water

FROSTING

16 tablespoons (2 sticks) unsalted butter, room temperature (take it out of the refrigerator when you turn the oven on)

4 cups (480 g) confectioners' sugar

½ cup (48 g) cocoa powder

¼ cup (60 ml) milk

2 teaspoons GF pure vanilla extract

½ teaspoon salt

TOOLS

Digital kitchen scale or measuring cups	Scissors	Oven mitts
Measuring spoons	Small bowl	Stand mixer, or handheld mixer and medium bowl
Two 8- or 9-inch (20 or 23 cm) round cake pans	Whisk	Large bowl
	Large bowl	Large plate
Parchment paper	Rubber spatula	Palette knife or butter knife
	Toothpick	

DO THE PREP

1 Preheat the oven to 350°F (180°C).

2 Grease the two cake pans with cooking spray and line the bottoms with parchment paper circles (see Tip).

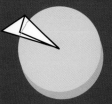

1 To make a square piece of parchment round, fold the paper in half, then fold it in half again to make a small square.

2 Now, fold it in half on the diagonal to make a triangle, then fold it in half on the diagonal one more time to make a long, skinny triangle.

3 Place the point of the triangle in the center of the cake pan and use a pencil to mark where the paper meets the edge of the pan.

4 Cut along your pencil mark and unfold the parchment paper. Voilà! You should have a round piece of parchment that matches the bottom of your pan.

DESSERT

*High-altitude adjustment: Use 2½ cups (313 g) GF all-purpose flour blend.

MAKE THE CAKE BATTER

3 In the small bowl, whisk together the flour, baking powder, xanthan gum, baking soda, and salt.

4 Add the granulated sugar, milk, cocoa powder, oil, eggs, and vanilla to the large bowl. Whisk to combine. Add the hot water and whisk again, slowly and carefully, until the mixture is completely smooth.

5 Add the flour mixture to the cocoa mixture and whisk until the batter is smooth.

BAKE AND COOL THE CAKE LAYERS

6 Pour the batter equally into the two prepared cake pans. Use the rubber spatula to scrape out the batter into the pans.

7 Put the cake pans in the oven, making sure they aren't touching. Bake for 40 to 45 minutes, until a toothpick inserted into the center of each cake comes out mostly clean. (A few little crumbs on the toothpick are OK.)

8 Wearing oven mitts, carefully remove the cake pans from the oven and set aside to cool to room temperature.

MAKE THE FROSTING

9 While the cakes are cooling, prepare the frosting. Add the butter to the bowl of the stand mixer, or the medium bowl if you're using a handheld mixer. Mix on medium-high speed until smooth, about 1 minute.

10 Add the confectioners' sugar, cocoa powder, milk, vanilla, and salt and mix on medium-high until very light and fluffy. If the frosting is too thick to spread easily, add an extra tablespoon of milk to thin it out.

FROST THE CAKE

11 When the cakes are completely cooled, turn one cake out of the pan onto a large plate and peel off the piece of parchment paper.

12 Top the cake with about ½ cup (135 g) of the frosting. Use the palette knife or butter knife to spread the frosting to the edges of the cake.

13 Turn the second cake pan over and let the cake fall out onto your hand. Peel off the parchment paper. Carefully place the cake right side up on the frosting-topped bottom cake.

14 Spread the rest of the frosting on the top and sides of the cake. Use a knife to cut the cake into wedges. Serve and enjoy!

MONSTER COOKIES

MAKES: 40 cookies **PREP TIME:** 15 minutes
COOK TIME: 60 minutes (about 12 minutes per batch)

No one's quite sure how these flourless cookies got their name, but everyone *does* agree that monster cookies are chock-full of goodness: oats, peanut butter, chocolate chips, and M&M candies. They're moist and chewy on the inside and slightly crispy around the edges.

• •

INGREDIENTS

1 cup (220 g) packed brown sugar

¾ cup (150 g) granulated sugar

8 tablespoons (1 stick) unsalted butter, room temperature (see page 12)

1½ cups (396 g) smooth peanut butter

2 teaspoons baking soda

2 teaspoons GF pure vanilla extract

½ teaspoon salt

3 large eggs

4½ cups (432 g) GF old-fashioned rolled oats

½ cup (100 g) mini M&Ms

½ cup (90 g) mini chocolate chips

TOOLS

Digital kitchen scale or measuring cups

Measuring spoons

Stand mixer, or handheld mixer and large bowl

2-tablespoon cookie scoop, or large spoon

Baking sheet

Oven mitts

Wire rack

DO THE PREP

1 Preheat the oven to 350°F (180°C).

MAKE THE DOUGH

2 Add the brown sugar, granulated sugar, and butter to the bowl of the stand mixer, or a large bowl if you're using a handheld mixer. Mix on medium speed until light and fluffy, about 2 minutes. (For a helpful picture, see Confetti Cupcakes, page 124.)

3 Add the peanut butter, baking soda, vanilla, and salt and mix to combine. Add the eggs and mix again.

4 Add the oats and mix until evenly incorporated. The dough will be very thick. Add the M&Ms and chocolate chips and mix to combine.

SHAPE AND BAKE THE DOUGH

5 Use the cookie scoop (or spoon) to portion out eight 2-tablespoon-size balls of dough. Place them 2 inches (5 cm) apart on a baking sheet. Put the baking sheet in the oven. Bake for 12 minutes, until the cookies are just set; they will still be soft.

DESSERT

6 Wearing oven mitts, carefully remove the baking sheet from the oven and set aside to cool for 5 minutes. Use the spatula to transfer the cookies to the wire rack to cool completely.

7 Repeat steps 5 and 6 until all of the cookies have been baked.

8 Store any uneaten cookies in an airtight container for up to 1 week.

SUGAR COOKIES

MAKES: 36 cookies   **PREP TIME:** 15 minutes   **COOK TIME:** 20 to 30 minutes (about 9 minutes per batch)

Every baker should have a great sugar cookie recipe at their disposal. These sweet, delicate cookies are great plain or with a lemony kick from the optional lemon zest.

*High-altitude adjustment: Use 3 cups (375 g) GF all-purpose flour blend.

DO THE PREP

1 Preheat the oven to 350°F (180°C).

MAKE THE DOUGH

2 Add 1¼ cups (250 g) of the sugar and the butter to the bowl of the stand mixer, or a large bowl if you're using a handheld mixer. Mix on medium speed until light and fluffy, about 2 minutes. (For a helpful picture, see Confetti Cupcakes, page 124.)

3 Add the egg and vanilla and mix on low speed to combine.

4 In the small bowl, whisk together the flour, xanthan gum, baking soda, baking powder, salt, and the lemon zest, if you're using it.

5 Add the flour mixture to the butter mixture and mix on low speed until combined. Stop the mixer and scrape down the side of the bowl with the rubber spatula. Mix again on medium speed for a few seconds, until the dough is smooth and completely mixed.

SHAPE AND BAKE THE COOKIES

6 Add the remaining ¼ cup (50 g) sugar to the small bowl you used to mix the flour. Use the cookie scoop or spoon to scoop tablespoon-size balls of the dough, roll them between the palms of your hands, then roll them in the sugar.

7 Place the balls about 2 inches (5 cm) apart on a baking sheet. Bake the cookies for 8 to 9 minutes, until the tops are flat with a cracked surface and the bottom edges are slightly golden brown.

8 Wearing oven mitts, carefully remove the baking sheet from the oven and set aside to cool for a few minutes. Use the spatula to transfer the cookies to the wire rack to cool completely.

9 Repeat steps 6 through 8 with the remaining dough until all of the cookies are baked.

10 After the cookies are cooled, store them in an airtight container.

DESSERT

CHOCOLATE COOKIE ICE CREAM SANDWICHES

MAKES: 12 cookie sandwiches   **PREP TIME:** 15 minutes
COOK TIME: 20 minutes (about 10 minutes per batch)   **COOL AND ASSEMBLE TIME:** 20 minutes

Take your favorite brand of vanilla ice cream and sandwich it between freshly baked, perfectly chewy chocolate cookies. The result—these ice cream sandwiches—is pure heaven.

INGREDIENTS

10 tablespoons (1 stick plus 2 tablespoons) unsalted butter, room temperature (see page 12)

½ cup (108 g) packed brown sugar

½ cup (100 g) granulated sugar

1 teaspoon GF pure vanilla extract

1 large egg

1 cup plus 2 tablespoons (140 g) GF all-purpose flour blend*

¼ cup plus 2 tablespoons (36 g) cocoa powder

1 teaspoon xanthan gum

½ teaspoon baking soda

½ teaspoon salt

3 cups (420 g) vanilla ice cream

*High-altitude adjustment: Use 1¼ cups (156 g) GF all-purpose flour blend.

TOOLS

Digital kitchen scale or measuring cups

Measuring spoons

Stand mixer, or handheld mixer and medium bowl

Small bowl

Whisk

Rubber spatula

1-tablespoon cookie scoop, or spoon

Baking sheet

Oven mitts

Wire rack

Spatula

¼-cup (60 ml) ice cream scoop, or spoon

DO THE PREP

1 Preheat the oven to 350°F (180°C).

MAKE THE COOKIES

2 Add the butter, brown sugar, granulated sugar, and vanilla to the bowl of the stand mixer, or a medium bowl if you're using a handheld mixer. Mix everything together on medium speed until light and fluffy, about 2 minutes. (For a helpful picture, see Confetti Cupcakes, page 124.)

3 Add the egg and mix on low speed to combine.

4 In the small bowl, whisk together the flour, cocoa powder, xanthan gum, baking soda, and salt.

5 Add the flour mixture to the butter mixture and mix on low speed until everything is mostly mixed together, about 30 seconds. Stop the mixer and scrape down the sides of the bowl with the rubber spatula. Mix again on medium speed until completely combined, about 30 seconds more.

6 Use the cookie scoop or spoon to scoop out tablespoon-size balls of cookie dough. Place the balls about 2 inches (5 cm) apart on the baking sheet.

7 Put the baking sheet in the oven. Bake for 9 to 10 minutes, until the cookies are a little puffy, the edges are slightly wrinkly, and the tops look cracked.

8 Wearing oven mitts, carefully remove the baking sheet from the oven and set aside to cool for 5 minutes. Use the spatula to transfer the cookies to the wire rack to cool completely.

9 Repeat steps 6 through 8 until all the cookies are baked. You should have 24 cookies.

ASSEMBLE THE SANDWICHES AND ENJOY

10 When the cookies are completely cool, scoop about ¼ cup (35 g) vanilla ice cream onto one cookie, then top it with a second cookie. Repeat until all the cookies are made into sandwiches.

11 Serve and enjoy right away before the ice cream melts, or put them in a container in the freezer for later!

COOKIE PIZZA

MAKES: one 11-inch (28 cm) pizza (16 slices)   **PREP TIME:** 15 minutes
COOK TIME: 18 minutes   **DECORATE TIME:** 10 minutes

What's better than a freshly baked, still-warm chocolate chip cookie?
Answer: A *giant* chocolate chip cookie the size of a pizza!

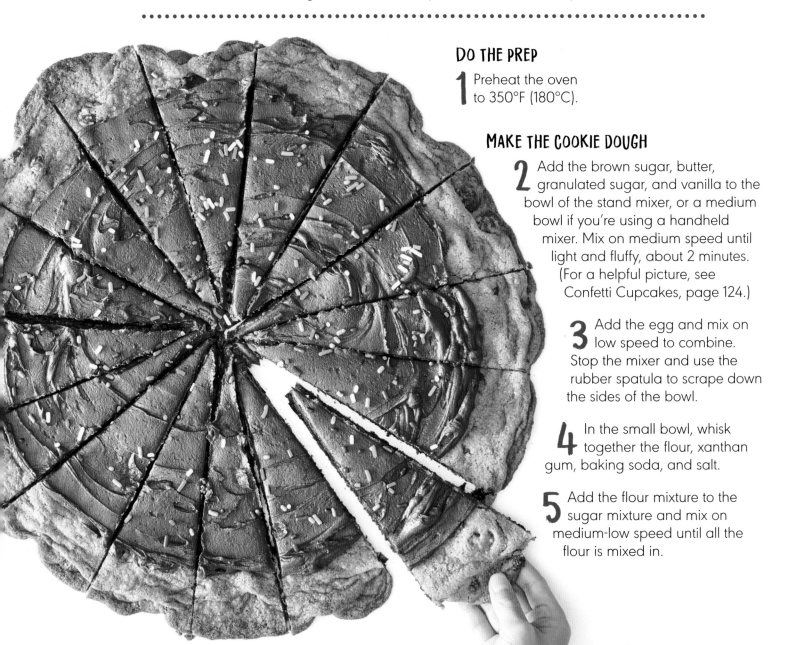

DO THE PREP

1 Preheat the oven to 350°F (180°C).

MAKE THE COOKIE DOUGH

2 Add the brown sugar, butter, granulated sugar, and vanilla to the bowl of the stand mixer, or a medium bowl if you're using a handheld mixer. Mix on medium speed until light and fluffy, about 2 minutes. (For a helpful picture, see Confetti Cupcakes, page 124.)

3 Add the egg and mix on low speed to combine. Stop the mixer and use the rubber spatula to scrape down the sides of the bowl.

4 In the small bowl, whisk together the flour, xanthan gum, baking soda, and salt.

5 Add the flour mixture to the sugar mixture and mix on medium-low speed until all the flour is mixed in.

6 Stop the mixer again and scrape down the sides of the bowl with the rubber spatula. Add the chocolate chips. Mix on low speed until the chocolate chips are evenly distributed.

SHAPE AND BAKE THE COOKIE PIZZA

7 Place a 15-inch (38 cm) square piece parchment paper on the baking sheet. Use the rubber spatula to scrape all the dough onto the center of the parchment paper. Place a second square of parchment paper on top of the dough and press the dough out into a 10-inch (25 cm) circle. (The second piece of parchment paper stops the dough from sticking to your hand. Compost or discard the second piece of parchment.)

8 Put the baking sheet in the oven. Bake for 18 minutes, until the top is crackly and golden brown all over.

9 Wearing oven mitts, carefully remove the baking sheet from the oven and slide the parchment paper with the cookie pizza onto the wire rack. Allow the cookie pizza to cool to room temperature.

MAKE THE FROSTING

10 While the cookie pizza is cooling, add the butter, confectioners' sugar, cocoa, milk, vanilla, and salt to the stand mixer or medium bowl. Mix on medium-high speed until light and fluffy, about 3 minutes.

TOP AND SERVE THE COOKIE PIZZA

11 When the cookie pizza is completely cooled, use the palette knife or butter knife to spread the chocolate frosting on the cookie pizza. Top with the sprinkles, if you like.

12 Slide the cookie pizza from the parchment paper onto the cutting board. Compost or throw away the parchment paper. Use the serrated knife to slice the cookie pizza into 16 wedges, then serve and enjoy.

INGREDIENTS

COOKIE PIZZA

½ cup (108 g) packed brown sugar

8 tablespoons (1 stick) unsalted butter, room temperature (see page 12)

¼ cup (50 g) granulated sugar

½ teaspoon GF pure vanilla extract

1 large egg

1 cup plus 2 tablespoons (140 g) GF all-purpose flour blend*

1 teaspoon xanthan gum

½ teaspoon baking soda

½ teaspoon salt

1 cup (170 g) chocolate chips

FROSTING AND TOPPING

4 tablespoons (½ stick) unsalted butter, room temperature (take it out of the refrigerator when you turn the oven on)

1 cup (120 g) confectioners' sugar

2 tablespoons cocoa powder

1 tablespoon milk

½ teaspoon GF pure vanilla extract

Pinch of salt

Sprinkles, optional

TOOLS

Digital kitchen scale or measuring cups

Measuring spoons

Stand mixer, or handheld mixer and medium bowl

Rubber spatula

Small bowl

Whisk

Parchment paper

Baking sheet

Oven mitts

Wire rack

Palette knife or butter knife

Cutting board

Serrated knife

DESSERT

*High-altitude adjustment: Use 1¼ cups (156 g) GF all-purpose flour blend.

135

BROWNIES

MAKES: 16 brownies   PREP TIME: 10 minutes   COOK TIME: 30 minutes

A little chewy, a little fudgy, and totally tasty—these brownies are the real deal.
If you like smooth brownies, leave out the chocolate chips. If you like the extra texture,
add them in. When you're the chef, you get to decide!

INGREDIENTS

GF nonstick cooking spray

1 cup (216 g) packed brown sugar

1 cup (125 g) GF all-purpose flour blend*

¾ cup (150 g) granulated sugar

⅔ cup (64 g) cocoa powder

1 teaspoon salt

½ teaspoon baking powder

1 cup (180 g) chocolate chips, optional

8 tablespoons (1 stick) unsalted butter, melted (see page 12; make sure the butter is just warm—hot butter will scramble the eggs)

3 large eggs

2 teaspoons GF pure vanilla extract

TOOLS

Digital kitchen scale or measuring cups

Measuring spoons

9-inch (23 cm) square baking pan

Large bowl

Whisk

Small bowl

Rubber spatula

Oven mitts

DO THE PREP

1 Preheat the oven to 350°F (180°C).

2 Grease the baking pan with cooking spray.

MAKE THE BATTER

3 In the large bowl, whisk together the brown sugar, flour, granulated sugar, cocoa powder, salt, and baking powder. Whisk in the chocolate chips, if you want.

4 In the small bowl, whisk the butter, eggs, and vanilla until completely mixed.

5 Add the butter mixture to the cocoa mixture and whisk until smooth. The batter will be thick, but keep whisking and it will come together.

6 Using the rubber spatula, scrape the batter out of the bowl and spread it in the prepared baking pan. Smooth the top with the rubber spatula.

BAKE THE BROWNIES

7 Put the baking pan in the oven. Bake for 30 minutes, until the edges are set and the center has a crackly top.

8 Wearing oven mitts, carefully remove the baking pan from the oven.

9 Allow the brownies to cool to room temperature. Cut them into 16 squares with a knife and serve. (They'll be much easier to cut when they've cooled completely.)

*High-altitude adjustment: Use 1 cup plus 2 tablespoons (141 g) GF all-purpose flour blend.

CHAI MARSHMALLOWS

MAKES: about 36 marshmallows **COOK TIME:** 45 minutes **COOL TIME:** 4 hours

If you think marshmallows only come in one flavor, think again! These soft, fluffy marshmallows are infused with the warm cinnamon, ginger, cardamom, and clove flavors of chai tea. You won't ever see marshmallows the same way! These are so delicious you will want to eat them by themselves as a sweet treat. This is a more-advanced recipe that involves working with hot sugar. Ask for help from an adult. Then enjoy the end result!

• •

INGREDIENTS

1 cup (240 ml) water

3 decaffeinated chai tea bags

2 cups (400 g) granulated sugar

¼ cup (60 ml) corn syrup

2 tablespoons plus 1 teaspoon unflavored gelatin (three ¼-ounce/7 g envelopes)

⅛ teaspoon salt

GF nonstick cooking spray

½ cup (60 g) confectioners' sugar

TOOLS

Liquid measuring cup or mug

Digital kitchen scale or measuring cups

Medium saucepan

Candy thermometer, or small spoon and glass of cold water

Stand mixer with whisk attachment, or handheld mixer and large bowl

Spoon

9-inch (23 cm) square baking pan

Plastic wrap

Rubber spatula

Cutting board

Chef's knife or kitchen scissors

Small bowl

MAKE THE TEA

1 Heat the water in the saucepan on the stovetop over high heat until it comes to a boil. Remove the saucepan from the heat and pour ½ cup (120 ml) of the water into a liquid measuring cup or a mug. (Ask an adult to help you pour the hot water, if you need to.) Add the tea bags to the water in the measuring cup and allow to steep for 5 minutes.

MAKE THE MARSHMALLOW FLUFF

2 While the tea is steeping, add the granulated sugar and corn syrup to the remaining ½ cup (120 ml) hot water in the saucepan. Heat on the stovetop over medium-high heat, without stirring, until the mixture comes to a boil. Clip a candy thermometer to the side of the saucepan and boil the syrup, without stirring, until the syrup reaches 240°F (115°C). This should take about 10 minutes. (If you don't have a candy thermometer, use the spoon to drop a small amount of the sugar syrup into a glass of cold water. The sugar syrup should form a soft, sticky ball that can be flattened when you gently squeeze it between your thumb and pointer finger. This is called the "soft ball stage.")

3 While the sugar syrup is boiling, remove the tea bags from the hot water. Pour the tea into the bowl of the stand mixer or a large bowl if you're using a handheld mixer.

4 Sprinkle the gelatin on top of the tea and leave it to sit for about 5 minutes. If any gelatin doesn't get moistened by the liquid, use the back of a spoon to press it down until it's moist. Place the bowl on the mixer base and put the whisk attachment on the machine. Leave it until the sugar syrup reaches the right temperature.

5 Ask an adult for help with this step, especially if you are using a handheld mixer. When the sugar mixture is at 240°F (115°C), turn the mixer on to medium-low speed. Very carefully, remove the saucepan of hot sugar syrup from the heat and slowly pour the syrup down the side into the bowl.

(Don't pour hot syrup on the whisk attachment, or it may come flying out and burn you.) Add the salt.

6 Turn the mixer up to medium-high speed and whisk for 8 to 10 minutes, until the mixture is very fluffy and glossy and the outside of the bowl feels just barely warm when you touch it. Turn off the mixer.

SHAPE THE MARSHMALLOWS

7 Line the baking pan with plastic wrap. Spray the rubber spatula with cooking spray.

8 Use the spatula to scrape the marshmallow mixture into the baking pan, spread it to the edges in an even layer, and make the surface as smooth as you can.

9 Dust the surface with a thin layer of the confectioners' sugar. Allow the marshmallows to cool completely at room temperature, at least 4 hours.

10 Dust the cutting board with a light coating of confectioners' sugar. Flip the marshmallow out of the baking pan and onto the cutting board. Peel off the plastic wrap.

11 Spray the chef's knife or scissors with cooking spray. Cut the marshmallows into 36 pieces, each 1½ inches (4 cm) square. Add the marshmallows a few at a time to a small bowl with the remaining confectioners' sugar and toss them to coat. Store in an airtight container for up to 1 month.

DESSERT

MASCARPONE WITH BERRIES

MAKES: 4 servings **PREP TIME:** 10 minutes

The rich creaminess of Italian mascarpone cheese, mild sweetness from a touch of honey and vanilla, and fresh, bright flavors of berries make this a delightfully light and refreshing dessert.

INGREDIENTS

- 8 ounces (225 g) mascarpone
- 2 tablespoons heavy cream
- 1 tablespoon honey
- 1 teaspoon GF pure vanilla extract
- 4 cups (500 to 750 g) fresh berries (quartered strawberries, or whole blueberries, raspberries, or blackberries)

TOOLS

Digital kitchen scale or measuring cups

Measuring spoons

Small bowl

Whisk

In the small bowl, whisk the mascarpone, heavy cream, honey, and vanilla until combined and smooth. Divide the berries among four bowls and spoon on dollops of the mascarpone mousse. Serve and enjoy.

DESSERT

LEMON GRANITA

MAKES: 4 servings **PREP TIME:** 10 minutes **FREEZE TIME:** about 5 hours

Originally from the island of Sicily in the Mediterranean Sea off the toe of Italy's boot, granita is equal parts sorbet, Italian ice, and slushy. It can be made with any kind of fruit juice, but the classic lemon is especially bright and refreshing. The trick is to be patient while you wait for the sugary ice crystals to develop.

MAKE THE SYRUP

1 Combine the water and sugar in the saucepan and heat on the stovetop over medium-high heat. Stir until the sugar dissolves, about 5 minutes.

2 Turn off the heat, move the sugar syrup to a cool burner, and let it cool.

3 Meanwhile, put the lemons on the cutting board and use the chef's knife to cut each in half along its equator. One at a time, put the lemon halves in the citrus juicer and squeeze out the juice into the liquid measuring cup until you have ⅔ cup (160 ml) juice. (If you don't have a citrus juicer, you can squeeze the lemons, cut side down, with your hand until the juice comes out.)

4 Add the lemon juice to the sugar syrup and stir to mix. Pour the mixture into the baking pan or baking dish and carefully place it in the freezer.

FREEZE AND SERVE

5 Freeze for 2 hours, until the mixture begins to crystallize around the edges. Take it out of the freezer, and scrape and stir the mixture with the fork, making sure to scrape down the sides, too.

6 Return the baking pan to the freezer. Stir and scrape again every hour for about 3 hours more, until the mixture is frozen into icy shards.

7 Once all the syrup has frozen into ice crystals, serve. Use a large spoon to scoop portions into cups or small bowls. The granita will melt quickly if it's left out of the freezer, so pop the baking pan back in as soon as you have scooped out all the servings you need.

INGREDIENTS

1¼ cups (300 ml) water

⅔ cup (133 g) sugar

4 lemons (⅔ cup/ 160 ml lemon juice)

TOOLS

Liquid measuring cup

Digital kitchen scale or measuring cups

Small saucepan

Spoon

Cutting board

Chef's knife (see Knives, page 8)

Citrus juicer, optional but recommended

9-inch (23 cm) square metal baking pan or shallow 2½ quart (2.5 L) glass baking dish

Fork

ACKNOWLEDGMENTS

We extend our deepest gratitude to the multitude of people who supported this book, made it possible, and made it better: to all the families who answered surveys that helped us decide which recipes to include in this cookbook; to our longtime publisher, The Experiment (especially Matthew, Olivia, Jennifer, Besse, Beth, Hannah, Emily, and Madeline); to our agent, Jenni Ferrari-Adler, and Union Literary; to our children, Marin, Charlotte, and Timothy; and to all the kid recipe testers who gave us amazing feedback: Audrey M, Ben H, Benjamin G, Connor E, Cormac E, Eliza W, Emelia E, Emma H, Ethan M, Henry W, John B, Lander W, Phoebe G, Sarah B, and Thomas B. Thank you!

INDEX

ABOUT THE AUTHORS

KELLI BRONSKI AND PETER BRONSKI are the parents of three kids who love to cook—Marin, Charlotte, and Timothy. Pete and Kelli are also the husband-and-wife cofounders of acclaimed food blog No Gluten, No Problem and coauthors of the popular cookbooks *No Gluten, No Problem Pizza*, *Artisanal Gluten-Free Cooking*, *Gluten-Free Family Favorites*, and *Artisanal Gluten-Free Cupcakes*. They've been developing gluten-free recipes since 2007, when Pete was diagnosed with celiac disease. They live in Colorado, where their household, their kitchen, and their meals are always gluten-free.

nogluten-noproblem.com

🅕 nogluten.noproblem

🅞 nogluten.noproblem

🅣 peterbronski

🅟 OfficialNGNP

🅨 NoGlutenNoProblem